MW01104944

I Lost Two Boobs
and
Gained Two Balls

*nice /
Thanks for
your support!
Gail*

I Lost Two Boobs
and
Gained Two Balls

One Woman's Journey to Finding Her Voice

GAIL ROGNAN

I LOST TWO BOOBS AND GAINED TWO BALLS
ONE WOMAN'S JOURNEY TO FINDING HER VOICE

Copyright © 2015 Gail Rognan.

All rights reserved. No part of this book may be used or reproduced by any means, graphic, electronic, or mechanical, including photocopying, recording, taping or by any information storage retrieval system without the written permission of the author except in the case of brief quotations embodied in critical articles and reviews.

iUniverse books may be ordered through booksellers or by contacting:

iUniverse
1663 Liberty Drive
Bloomington, IN 47403
www.iuniverse.com
1-800-Authors (1-800-288-4677)

Because of the dynamic nature of the Internet, any web addresses or links contained in this book may have changed since publication and may no longer be valid. The views expressed in this work are solely those of the author and do not necessarily reflect the views of the publisher, and the publisher hereby disclaims any responsibility for them.

Any people depicted in stock imagery provided by Thinkstock are models, and such images are being used for illustrative purposes only.
Certain stock imagery © Thinkstock.

ISBN: 978-1-4917-8029-9 (sc)
ISBN: 978-1-4917-8030-5 (e)

Library of Congress Control Number: 2015917336

Print information available on the last page.

iUniverse rev. date: 10/22/2015

This book is dedicated to Janice.
You taught me what it is to live well and what it is to die well.

TABLE OF CONTENTS

ACKNOWLEDGEMENTS

I couldn't have written this book without the support of my Women's Circle, my healing team, Carol Squire, Jane Palmer, Rebecca Ingalls, Roxanne Fairfax, Sheree Doll, Sharon Maynard, Dr. Leah Oman and Erika Kardly. Thank you to Betsy Zick for our "creative" days when you would paint and I would write. Thanks to Kathy Reed for the many hours she spent editing my book for me. I thank Kathy Plant for her continued support and editing. Thanks to Katie Brimhall for the final editing. But most of all, I couldn't have done this without God.

I have always felt that it is dishonest for an author to write an instructional guide for others without including some personal revelation about their own experience with the process they are talking about. Although my story may be far less inspirational than those people I have read about and whose journeys I have shared, I can confirm that I am endeavoring to live out these principles from my own experience. I trust that you will be able to interweave parts of your own story into mine.

Medical Advice

The information, ideas, and suggestions in this book are not intended as a substitute for professional medical advice. Before following any suggestions contained in this book, consult your physician. Neither the author nor the publisher shall be liable or responsible for any loss or damage allegedly arising as a consequence of your use or application of any information or suggestions in this book.

PROLOGUE

She wears many masks, some of which I know: Kick Ass, Little Girl, Lil' Beav, Artist and Mature Self. Sometimes I glimpse her in the faces I encounter: pale, dark, smooth, wrinkled, weeping. Laughing and crying out for peace, justice and healing.

She was there when life began, her light shown as the world unfolded. She weeps when we hurt each other and others; she tends to all of the wounded. She has a special place in her heart for Kick Ass, as she sees her spunk and the twinkle in her eyes.

I think of her often, especially now as we are healing. She will not force her way into our midst, but bides her time, and once invited, she will stand by us fiercely, like a mother with her cub.

All selves will join in to celebrate because she has returned and those who loved her without knowing her true name all through her long exile from home.

RELEASE

8-17-12 (written 2 months after my double mastectomy)
Bent over, double
Unable to stand straight
Or fully look up
The burden and I were one.
This cancer has released me
I stand tall
Knowing that I have not done evil
But that evil came upon me.
Not only is the burden taken from me
It is healed
My power and spirit are released.
I raise up my hands
My head thrown back
My eyes raised
I praise God.

INTRODUCTION

So I lost two boobs. So what! For me, cancer was not doable without humor. I am part of an obscure group who has had the honor of facing her mortality and it woke me up and made me a better, and a stronger, person.

It changed me.

After my diagnosis, I went into panic mode for about a week. Then I searched for a book that could guide me through the process of fighting cancer, with depth and humor that would give me hope and guidance throughout my journey. I could not find that book. I wanted to find others who believed in and followed alternative medicine and made a decision to live a life that supports quality of life versus standard-of-care.

I am a person who needs to tell stories and share the details of things I experience. But when I tell these stories, there is something missing. To clarify what I am trying to say, I need to write about it. I find great meaning in this.

I found most cancer books to be downers which followed the "standard of care" protocol I did not follow. Instead I wanted to read about and talk to women who triumphed over an evil that invaded their bodies, who had the balls to say, "You are not going to kill me you son-of-a-bitch!"

I read once that if you can't find the book you need, write that book yourself. So here I am writing the book I could not find.

Since humor helped me survive cancer, this book will contain some humor. Please understand I don't find anything funny about getting cancer and all that entails. But I find humor where there is none to be found in the most absurd situations. It helps me see the direst circumstances in a more palatable light. I use humor to get me through tough situations.

I also wanted to share the wisdom, strength, faith, resources and hope I found along the way, in myself and in others. I found that support for cancer survivors and especially for those choosing a more proactive, independent path was sorely lacking in the area I lived. So I also wanted to provide to others what was lacking for me. Most people I told about my cancer immediately told me about someone they knew who had died of cancer. (Note to reader: this is what NOT to do!)

Along the way, I learned some important lessons. I learned to speak up, set strong boundaries and become more fearless. In other words, I may have lost two boobs, but I did indeed grow two balls!

Let me make it clear from the start. When I talk about "balls," I am not talking about physical balls or testicles. I am not making a distinction about masculine or feminine, as females can have the kind of balls I am describing. Having a pair of balls represents an attitude, a state of mind and a way of thinking and being in the world.

I was lucky to find a female doctor who specialized in breast cancer. She was a godsend. The first time I met her, a week after I was diagnosed, she immediately grabbed my hand, looked me straight in the eyes and said, "This is not a death sentence. You are going to be okay." I believed her. It helped me relax so I could make better decisions for myself about treatment, and it helped me regain my spark and positive attitude. I hope this book provides these things for you and that you know that you are not alone on your journey.

Facing a series of crises led me to explore my spirituality and forced me to find a new way to bring coherence to my life. The crises threatened my identity and self-esteem, but they also broadened my horizon. It was both a time of danger and opportunity. I was ready to listen as I waited in the darkness.

The following fourteen chapters provide a structure, but not a system, for exploring a journey with cancer and how that affected my life and my spirituality. Just as one's spiritual journey circles around a quest for truth, this book will follow a non-linear flow. It offers descriptive, rather than a prescriptive approach on dealing with cancer. I have no advice to give. I hope this book serves the purpose of telling my story while still leaving spaces and room for questions.

I am still in the process of freeing myself enough to let myself be completely held in the safe embrace of God. But in many ways, I am allowing myself to move to the center. I am indeed on my way home. A place where the God of our unknowing, the God who can't be described in words, calls my name and says "You are my beloved, on you my favor rests." And, so, I am ready now to share my story. When, by God's grace, you have managed to save your life, you want to pass on what you have learned. I want to tell those who are lost, "There are things I did to find my way. Maybe some of them will help you find yours." As I share the story of how I saved my life, my wish is that there is some hope and consolation here to light your path through the darkness.

CHAPTER ONE

The Diagnosis

Wake Up Calls

In times of great destruction
Our lives depend on deep listening.
In the present moment,
We must listen to the wind
It carries the story of our unrest, pain and healing
The wind is a prophet.
If we continue to ignore the beauty that nature offers,
We will be covered in black muck
Unable to free ourselves
The flow of the spirit will be locked
Indefinitely.
Seen from the eyes of God
These destructions are the shocks needed
To wake us up.

I had my wake-up call at fifty-eight. The moment I heard "you have cancer," my life changed forever. I drove home in a daze while the world around me went on as it always does, as everyone around me had no idea of what I was dealing with. I could no longer pretend that the world would be okay again. I contacted my mom, my naturopath and my boss soon after I got home. Speaking of my disease out loud made it all seem more real.

I spent quite some time lying on my bed ranting at God and crying. I told God I no longer believed in Him and that I hated Him and asked him how he could have let this happen to me. I had dealt with so many losses and set-backs that I was done. I could no longer cope. I was at the end of my rope. Thomas Merton wrote a prayer that says, "My Lord God, I have no idea where I am going, I do not see the road ahead of me." What I was to realize later was this was the best place I could be: vulnerable and no longer in control.

I had no choice but to accept that all was hopeless and that I could no longer "fix" things. All I could do was surrender. When I did this, I felt God meet me right where I was- lost, scared and all alone. If that meant dying, then that is what I would have to accept. All I could do was ask for help getting through whatever was to come. I could no longer force things to be okay. I had to admit that my life was crap, but also that I was loved by God just as I was, broken and scared. Writing this book became the main way I stayed in this place of openness and acceptance so I would never go back to denial again. To never believe I am the one in control again.

Within a couple hours, I was researching on the internet about breast cancer and treatment which helped me calm down and feel like I was doing something. All I had left was having a shot at having a life where I was present, mindful and kind to myself and others, and I did not know how long that life would be. I was lucky to have the most common kind of breast cancer: infiltrating ductal carcinoma, which is about seventy percent of all breast cancer diagnoses. Mine was stage two and ended up in the margins of my right breast which required two surgeries the same week. Luckily, it had not traveled to my lymph nodes.

If this had happened ten years before, I probably would have taken to my bed and just given up on my life, feeling like I had been given a death sentence. So what had changed? My faith had matured and I had gained much confidence and resources. I was fortunate to explore my spirituality in a safe place with the help of a wise and competent spiritual director. A Zen saying "When the student is ready, the teacher will come" illustrates that our body, mind and spirit prepare us for each level of insight we experience. After developing some health problems, experiencing many failed relationships with men and going through my Dad's illness and death, I was ready to learn a new way of being.

During my work with the spiritual director, I also began doing some body work with an acupuncturist/Chinese doctor. It was this doctor who led me to my Eye Movement Desensitization and Reprocessing (EMDR) therapist who helped me deal with a life of emotional trauma and feelings of anxiety. She helped me deal with family issues using my right brain and this was exceptionally beneficial to me. I had a long history of difficulty and misunderstanding with my Dad before he died, and this therapy was what finally allowed me to heal from that. I also changed my diet drastically after realizing I did not do well with dairy, wheat and gluten.

All this emotional, physical and spiritual work on myself gave me an inner strength and resilience to deal more effectively with uncertainty. I developed a fierce desire to live and to make myself healthy and whole.

In her book *The Finishing School*, Gail Godwin describes two kinds of people:[1]

> *"One kind, you can tell just by looking at them at what point they congealed into their final selves. It might be a very nice self, but you know you can expect no more surprises from it. Whereas, the other kind keeps moving, changing. With these people, you can never say, "X stops here," or "Now I know all there is to know about Y." That doesn't mean they're unstable. Ah, no, far from it. They are fluid. They keep moving forward and making new trysts with life, and the motion of it keeps them young. In my opinion, they are the only people who are still alive."*

Spirals

I shall never cease exploration
When I reach the end of my exploring
I will arrive back where I began
And know it for the first time
I will know in my heart
That I finally belong there.

---

[1] Gail Godwin, *The Finishing School* (New York, NY: Random House, 1999), 254.

Two years before I was diagnosed with breast cancer, I made a decision to move to a more rural, quiet area where I could find a community of like-minded people. I was tired of living in a big city area with all the people, noise and traffic. I told two friends who I met with every few months about the kind of community and place I was visualizing. I even made a collage so they could see visually what I was looking for. My friend's eyes got big when she saw my collage and she pulled out a newspaper article about a nearby location. The article had every adjective I had described to my friends verbally and shown them visually. Right then and there, we planned a day-trip for the three of us to this island in about a month's time.

The minute I stepped on the island, I felt like I was "home." I felt calm and at peace and I knew that I needed to find a way to get here permanently. When we had lunch at a local restaurant, I grabbed a newspaper and started looking for a job. I had been teaching online as a college professor for the last six years at home and was tired of being so isolated. I knew I needed a job that got me out around people.

I saw an ad for an advertising representative for the local newspaper. When I got up the next day at home, I tracked down an old friend who I used to sell advertising with years ago as I knew she worked for the newspaper. What I didn't know is that she was the publisher of the paper and was the one hiring for the job. When I emailed her, she said "call me!" And I did! Within minutes I had emailed her my resume and we had set up an interview; a week after, I was offered the job. I still had an apartment where I currently lived and no place on the island, but I took the job knowing everything would fall into place. My first day at work, one of my co-workers took me to see an apartment her in-laws were willing to rent by the night. It was a cute place so I told them I wanted to start renting it the next night.

For about three weeks, I commuted from my current home on Friday after work and took the ferry back to the island on Monday mornings. I would pack on weekends. It was an extremely stressful time (not a good thing for cancer I would find out later), especially since I was also learning a new job and knew no one on the island except for the friend I had contacted about the job. I continued to teach online part-time for the next year.

I finally moved full-time to the island after a few weeks and my landlords asked if I would like the apartment full-time. I said yes and hired a moving company to move my possessions.

I lived with this busy schedule for almost a year and a half, until I finally gave my notice at the university I taught for. But the job at the newspaper was stressful enough for two jobs. They kept firing my co-workers for one reason or another and the work would always come back onto me until they hired and trained someone else. It would take months for the new person to get up to speed, which left the burden on me. Then the new person would quit or get fired. Finally, I went to my boss and told her I would quit unless they either found me some permanent help, or lessen my client load and pay me more.

I gave them another two months and they did not do what I had asked. So I quit. I gave them a month's notice and started planning what I would do for money when I left. During that time, the publisher came back to me and asked me to stay. I told her I would only do it if I could have Mondays off, and that they needed to hire someone to take some of my clients. She accepted my offer and I ended up staying.

Looking back, I now see God's hand in all of this. I couldn't have known that two months later I would be diagnosed with breast cancer and would need health insurance to pay for my medical care.

I had been faithful in getting mammograms every two years since I was about forty years old. With my move and all the stress in my life, I put off my mammogram for an extra year or so. For some reason, I kept cancelling my appointment and re-scheduling. I think deep down, I knew something was amiss, although I had no symptoms and did not feel a lump in either breast on self-exams.

When I finally did get the mammogram, I figured it would turn out just like every other one and I would be fine. But the next day, I got a call from the hospital saying they wanted me to come in for a second mammogram. I thought this was odd and asked why. The woman said they had compared the film to the last picture taken of me three years ago and something in my right breast looked different.

I began to get a bit anxious, but most of all I was pissed. I was a busy woman and did not have time for all this. I found myself judging the technician who did the mammograms figuring she was not very skilled as she did not work for a big hospital like we had in the city I had lived in. It turns out she was very skilled and I owe her my life.

Someone once asked me if I was happy that I got cancer. I had to think about that for a while before giving an honest answer. I told them that I don't think I was ever happy about it but I was learning that I could feel joy even in the most difficult, depressing situations.

The joy for me comes from not having to push through anymore. Being such a driven person all my life, I always had some goal I felt I had to pursue whether it was good for me or not. I didn't have a very balanced life, as I was a workaholic. I was taught from a young age to work hard and not be lazy so it was hard for me to relax for long. After a while, I forgot what it was to have fun. A friend of mine tried to give some ideas on how to have fun and they seemed forced and foreign to me.

I would feel a desire try to renew my spirit, relax or just hang out. So I would schedule some kind of retreat for a few days. For a while, it helped. Until I got back into the same old grind. I even spent a couple days of every year for about five years with some nuns at a priory retreat center. There were no phones or television. I slept on an uncomfortable single bed but I slept well. It was wonderful and the effects lasted for some time.

Once I got cancer, I could no longer pretend that the life I was living was working. I had to step back and think about what kind of life I really wanted. If I was tired, then I needed to take a break. Take a walk and take in the healing energy of nature. Feel the warm smile of a friend. Laugh. Or smile at a stranger. Spend more time with animals who I adore. I had to make my life one long retreat. I had to redefine what work and success were for me.

I think that like a lot of other people, I got lost along the way. I became the center of my universe and in control of every aspect of my life. How dare breast cancer disrupt my plans! But this was God's way of getting my attention. I had ignored previous attempts, not as serious as this time, so I went back to my old way of doing things.

If I got stuck off center, I wanted to stop trying to force the solution. It means learning to live through uncertainty knowing that the answer will come if you just wait. Easy to say and so hard to do. It means backing off until the answer emerges naturally from a place of peace and natural instinct within me (what I call my God place). Lighten up. Loosen up. Go with the flow.

> Kahul Gibran, *The Prophet,* says:
> "Your joy is your sorrow unmasked …
> The deeper that sorrow carves into your heart the more joy
> you can contain.
>
> When you are joyless, look deep into your heart and you shall
> find it is only that which has given you sorrow that is giving
> you joy. When you are sorrowful look again into your heart,
> and you shall see that in truth you are weeping for that which
> has been delight."[2]

The way I interpret this is that when you open your heart to love and life, you accept the possibility of loss and pain. When we face our mortality, life becomes less fearful and we can choose to spend whatever time we have experiencing as much joy as we can.

Surrender

I struggled so mightily,
The stress
The strain
The confusion Cycled around
I got stuck in the center.
A glimpse of the Divine comes through
The cracks of the resolve that I grasp onto so fiercely. I reach
the bottom

---

[2] Kahlil Gibran. *The Prophet* (New York, NY: Alfred & Knopp, 1923). 129.

I run out of reserves
I am lost
I am tired
I am out of ideas.
That is when I finally let go of control
I surrender to your will God
What is meant to be, will be
I turn it all over to you
I trust completely that whatever is for my highest good
Will come to pass.

In a way, my diagnosis was somewhat a relief for me, as getting cancer had always been one of my biggest fears. Once I got it, I didn't have to be afraid of getting it anymore. I just had to find a way to manage it. So the moment I found out I had cancer was the moment I first started letting go of control.

I had spent all my life believing that if I could remain in control, nothing bad could happen to me. How wrong that was. So I realized I might as well let go of control and face whatever life brought.

I could choose to accept that I had cancer and deal with it, or give up all hope and just let myself die. I knew I had to "give in" and accept the greater life God had planned for me. The years of struggle to ward off death led to burn out as I denied parts of myself that I deemed unworthy. I could now see that that was killing me and had possibly played a part in the creation of the disease that I had been afraid of all my life.

Now I had to face the truth and admit I was vulnerable just like everyone else. I needed love and support. I needed God.

Sharing the News

I am a very private person, but I knew from the start I could not do this alone. The more support I had, the better. So I confided in some people at work while I was waiting to hear my diagnosis. Once I got it, I let my boss know first. She and I shared a special relationship, as she was a cancer survivor and I could share my fears and concerns with her and ask her questions. I also shared with a few close friends who were also clients, my mom and my naturopath. Telling my mom was the hardest, as she does not handle bad news well. She gets very anxious and that makes me feel more anxious so I avoid talking to her unless I am able to have a superficial conversation. I also called my former therapist as she is a breast cancer survivor. She offered to see me for free for a few sessions of therapy. Luckily it was covered by insurance so I started seeing her twice a month only a few weeks after my surgery.

Using Humor as a Way to Cope

I am sure most people don't equate cancer with humor and I was a bit surprised myself that my humor surfaced so quickly on my journey. I found the more that I could laugh, make jokes, get others to laugh, the less stress I felt and the more positive and hopeful I was of my prognosis. It put others at ease. It can also improve immune function. My doctor often would comment on how she believed I was doing so well because of my positive attitude. She was all for me writing this book and loved the title.

The thing is, if you spend your life as a positive and optimistic person, there is a good chance these qualities will emerge during your cancer experience. I wondered why more people were not willing to share about their struggles. I found the best thing for me was to not hide the fact that I had cancer and, instead be totally open and transparent about it. I did have to be careful around some people as they tended to want to tell me how to run my life and manage my disease, even thought they had never had cancer themselves. There were some that did not appreciate my humor or honesty, so I had to listen for cues from each person as to how they might handle it. On the other side of this, I also wanted to surround myself with people who shared my humor and could handle my honesty. Those that couldn't were not as welcome in my life. When it comes down to it, it is a matter of life and death on how you handle disease. If you don't let it ruin your humor, if you are choosier on who you let into your life, it helps you have the strength you need to survive. I felt that as long as I could keep my cancer "happy" (or inactive, dormant), I could continue to live a happy, cancer-free life.

Gail Rognan

How the Diagnosis Changed Me

Cancer was a good thing in my life. It sounds strange but it was the physical manifestation of the lessons I needed to learn in my life. It was a new chapter that allowed me to be myself and to voice my opinions no matter the consequence. I decided from then on to not worry about being polite or what people thought of me. I was going to say exactly what I thought. I was in sales at the time, so I had to hold back at times and put on some false cheer. But the days I could not bear to be "fake" I would plan a day of visiting my favorite clients with whom I could be myself. Luckily, many of my clients fit this description. I would go into one client's office (who is also a friend) with a red gummy bear in my nose and ask her for a Kleenex. I thought she was going to fall out of her chair.

Another client (who became a good friend) would always ask me how I was. If I was having a bad day, I could tell her. I could even cry. She went through all my stages with me and celebrated the triumph of me coming out the other side cancer-free.

I allowed the newspaper I worked for to write a story about my journey as a way to gain support and also to help others going through the same thing.

Later, I would find out that cancer takes years, if not decades, to grow inside us. So even though I had turned my life around in many healthy ways, it was too late to stop the cancerous cells from growing to the point that a tumor resulted. I do believe my good habits kept the cancer at bay longer than most people's. But I was also missing keys element in my life that promoted the growth of the tumor which I will discuss later. I also see how the years of accumulated stress set me up to get cancer. But I felt like I could handle stress and I would be fine.

CHAPTER TWO

Taking an Active Role -
The Treatment - Losing a Few Boobs

It didn't take a long time of being in the healthcare system to realize that I did not agree with or understand much of it. I did, however, encounter several angels within the system that made my journey smoother. After I was called a few days following my first mammogram and told I needed to get another one plus to be prepared to get a biopsy the same day, depending on the results, a friend offered to drive me there and stayed with me during the whole thing. He took the day off from work to do this. The two nurses who were in the room during my procedure came up close to each side of me and held my hands so tight it almost hurt. But I was so grateful and it helped ease my fear and pain. I must warn those who experience this journey that you are required to get a third mammogram *after* the biopsy. It is painful and messy. You have bandages and ice around your chest as your breasts are compressed in the machine. Not fun.

I waited a week to get the results as my doctor was on vacation. I scheduled the earliest morning appointment I could to hear as soon as possible, but was kept waiting in the doctor's office for over a half an hour which just increased my anxiety. I let the nurse know I was upset by this. The doctor was very upfront and got right to the news that I indeed did have cancer and told me the steps I would need to take. I was in such a fog I could not take it all in. I should have taken a friend with me, but I was trying to be the strong, stoic person who did not need help or support. I do remember the doctor giving me a hug before she left the exam room.

I did not hear back right away from my doctor's office on who they were recommending that I see regarding surgery, so I called them and told them I wanted a referral by the end of the day. They got back to me within an hour. I found that you have to be assertive and follow up and not rely on anyone for your care. My balls were starting to show themselves a bit.

When I got an MRI, I dealt with a scheduler who was extraordinary. I had to take time off work to go off island to get my MRI and just before I was to go get the test, the machine broke down and I had to reschedule. The scheduler was so apologetic, kind and accommodating about it even though the MRI staff seemed to think it was no big deal and could care less that I was majorly inconvenienced. My scheduler actually sent me a card and gift card for a free coffee at the hospital cafeteria.

On the day I rescheduled, I did not know I should have asked my doctor for a tranquilizer. I got about two-thirds through the procedure and panicked. I was face down with my breasts sticking trough two slots and the MRI tech told me to stay still while she injected my breasts with dye. I could not continue. All I can compare it to was what it must feel like if you were buried alive and could not get out of the confined space. I told the MRI tech that I needed to get out of the machine and she argued with me that I could not because I was almost done. At that point, I freaked out even more, and screamed at her to "GET ME OUT NOW!" She did. She was not happy with me but I couldn't have cared less. I left my scheduler a message thanking her for her kindness and let her know what happened and told her she was an angel on earth. I was never charged for my MRI and I believe that the scheduler was behind this.

I didn't know how claustrophobic I was and the MRI made that even worse. I actually had to get counseling just to get over the trauma from this event.

What I found out later was that MRI is part of the "standard-of-care" protocol that doctors are required to prescribe for breast cancer. I told my doctor I was willing to go through surgery without the MRI results, as I refused to go through another.

Soon after I was diagnosed, I started doing research and asking my breast cancer surgeon/doctor questions so I could make an informed decision on my treatment. I had no intention of just blindly following any doctor's advice, even though I trusted my doctor immediately. I knew I had to make a decision that worked for me and made sure my doctor would support whatever decision I made, even if she didn't agree with it.

I had been interested in alternative health care for years and had been seeing a naturopath for almost twenty-two years before all this happened. My dad had a bad reaction to anesthesia during a minor operation, had cardiac arrest and went brain dead about fourteen years before my diagnosis, so I was very wary of doctors and hospitals. I decided on a double mastectomy after discovering that often the cancer travels from one breast to the other. I could not see getting a lumpectomy in my right breast followed by seven weeks of radiation (while trying to also work) and then having to go through the same thing with the left breast later. The surgery gave me peace of mind and I wanted the foreign substance out of my body as soon as possible. I am now convinced that the surgery caused errant cancer cells not removed to travel throughout my body but I can't worry about it. I still feel that the surgeries were the right treatment for me as I could not live with the thought of a foreign substance growing inside me. I needed to get it out. All I can do now is build my immune system up and manage the cancer as best I can the rest of my life using the tools I have learned to possibly reverse the cancer and stop it from coming back, which I will talk about later. It also gave me time to come up with a plan to get myself healthy. I felt the diagnosis, tests and surgery went so fast, I didn't have much time to process the whole experience.

I knew I would never agree to chemotherapy as I knew it also killed healthy cells and can cause many problems in one's body. I knew I would not withstand being sick from poisons put into my body. It went against everything I believed in. I chose quality of life even if it meant a shorter life. I may have agreed to radiation if it had not been for seven weeks off-island. I could not have kept my job if I'd taken that much time off. But after I researched radiation more, I would not even do that if given the option in the future, as it is a direct cause of cancer. Even the x-rays the dentist does can cause cancer so I now refuse to get them.

Taking an Active Role

My style is to get the facts, identify my choices and the consequences, network with people who have experienced the same thing, establish a support system that would support whatever decision I made, and then make the decision. But in the end, I based my decision on what my intuition was telling me and decided against using any conventional treatments after getting my surgeries done. I believe that God led me to the right doctor and treatment for me.

As far as what type of decision-maker I am, I am a combination of a deliberator and delayer. I delayed my decision until I felt I had enough information to make the right one for me after talking with my doctor and others who had been through this process. Once I felt I had enough information, I prayed about it and asked God to show me the right way. It only took about two weeks until I made the decision to get a double mastectomy rather than a lumpectomy of my right breast followed by radiation.

I used a strategy, considered the risks and did not look back. I was willing to go against popular or professional opinions to get the treatment I knew was right for me. I was blessed to have a doctor that supported my decisions. She preferred that I follow the standard of care protocol but when I went a different way, she supported that. She acted more as a consultant than a dictator. Months after my surgery, I found out that my doctor had breast cancer herself and was getting treatment. When I met up with her after she was back at work, she was a different person. She told me that she no longer told people what to do as she realized that each person has to find the right path for themselves. It changed the way she saw everything and has made her an even better doctor and person.

The skills I had gained in the professional world helped me in my research process and networking abilities. I had been through enough uncertainty and life experiences to know myself and what I could and could not withstand.

Once I made the decision, I felt very little conflict or uncertainty. I knew this option would give me the most peace of mind. At fifty-eight, I did not care that much if I lost my breasts. They were too large and I never liked them much anyway.

As far as I was concerned cutting off both breasts *was* my treatment and it was enough as far as dealing with conventional medicine. Later, I found a title for the route I chose: Integrated (or Blended) Care. I used the conventional method of surgery and supplemented that with alternative methods such as body (EMDR and Somatic) therapy, acupuncture, essiac tea and supplements, massage, nutrition, exercise and taking supplements. I also found a naturopath close to where I lived who gave me blood tests to check to see how I was doing. I refused to take tamoxifen as I knew it can cause brain and other kinds of cancers and many other problems. In short, I did whatever I could to build up my immune system as I knew this was my best defense in keeping the cancer from re-occurring.

When my right breast kept draining after the drain was removed, my doctor, who is also a surgeon, was quick to suggest another surgery to correct the problem. I told her that I wanted to wait and try some other things first. I worked with my acupuncturist, who is a Chinese doctor, doing acupuncture treatments and tinctures. Within about a month, the issue was resolved. If I had gotten another surgery, the after effects of anesthesia and the chance of more cancer cells dispersing around my body post-surgery would have caused more problems.

The benefits of any treatment need to be weighed against the risks. For example, for early stage breast cancer the potential for premature death and reduced quality of life are the risks when undergoing conventional cancer treatments. These treatments treat symptoms not the cause, and do not look at the whole person. There is an underlying imbalance that must be reversed. Getting chemotherapy does not reverse the imbalance and can, in fact, cause more problems. The cancer will most likely come back eventually unless the imbalance is reversed by a drastic change in lifestyle. Many people are declared cancer-free five years after finishing chemotherapy, but cancer can return because the chemotherapy caused cancer to grow.

My hospital stay confirmed my feelings that the medical care system needed changing, although the care I received was good. I was in the hospital for five days. I thought I would be able to go home the next day after my mastectomy, but more cancer was found in the margins, so I had a second surgery three days after my first surgery to get it out. I went home the day after my second surgery. But just five days in the hospital was very depressing. I felt isolated, hooked up to an IV line, and at first I needed to request for everything, including a bed pan. I was used to being independent and in control and it was very hard to remain positive and dignified. I feel for people who have long-term hospital stays and multiple surgeries to endure.

Before my surgery, and even when I was in the hospital recuperating, I started reading everything I could find on how to heal myself naturally and so I could understand the causes of cancer and how to reverse it. When your immune system is strong, the cancer can't survive or multiply. I learned that mind, body and spirit are inseparable and when we feel empowered, our immune system is empowered.

I learned what feeds cancer and stayed away from it – sugar, red meat with hormones in it (or chicken for that matter). I only eat organic, free- range meats and chicken. I know there are toxins in the plastic bottles water comes in so I only drink water from glass containers or safe plastic containers. I eat primarily as a vegetarian with occasional meals with healthy meat or chicken.

I took an online nutrition class which teaches you how diet can either cause inflammation to cause illness or help inflammation do what it is supposed to do: heal our wounds and correct things in our body when it is out of whack.

When we take drugs to stop pain caused by inflammation, our bodies don't know what to do. The natural process is thwarted and the inflammation is driven deeper into the body and becomes harmful. At some point, the inflammation becomes chronic and our bodies turn on themselves and start attacking healthy cells, which results in any number of illnesses, including cancer. There has to be billions of these unhealthy cells before cancer is evident.

The turning point in my attitude toward cancer was the first day I met my surgeon a week after my diagnosis. I went from fearing for my life to knowing that I would be okay just by the way she approached me. She looked me right in the eyes, held my hand and told me I was going to be fine. I believed her. This did tons to help me relax and clear out my foggy brain and make better decisions.

How I Changed My Life

Once I was waiting for my diagnosis, after my biopsy, I started drastically changing my life. I started taking food-grade H202 baths (to give my cells oxygen, which cancer does not like); I ordered essiac tea and started on the full program to build my immune system.

Nutrition

I changed my diet even more drastically than it had been. I had taken away gluten, wheat, dairy and soy over seven years before my diagnosis. I cut out all sugar and mostly ate as a vegetarian. I started doing cleanses on every major organ every six months for clearing toxins and parasites out of my body. I also take supplements in order to detoxify and keep disease away which included B-6, Dim-complex (a natural alternative to tamoxifen), adrenal complex, curcumin (turmeric), quercetin, milk thistle, green tea extract, tyrosine supplement, digestive enzymes, probiotics, B12, B- complex, COQ1O, shark liver oil, zeolite, vitamin D3, melatonin and resveratrol. I also do a Vitamin C flush once a month.

Physical

I started walking a bit each day with my dog, Spark, a few weeks after surgery. I increased walking distance after about three months. About six months after my surgery, I started taking a Razzl Dance class, then started training for a flash mob about three months before the actual mob. I continued with the individual yoga sessions I had started before I was diagnosed but I soon found a group of other cancer survivors to do yoga with. To date, I am now walking 30-60 minutes a day.

Spiritual

I had to look at my relationship with God and see why I still felt separate from Him.

Mental (Attitude)

I have always had a positive attitude but it was put to the test when I was diagnosed with cancer. There is a strong desire to live inside of me that I have had to access over and over in my life, but it took digging a bit deeper this time. I have a strong faith and sense of humor that get me through pretty much anything after periods of feeling scared or depressed. I developed a tough-minded; warrior attitude after being diagnosed that has not left me. Since I made the decision to live life to the fullest, my life has become precious and I guard it daily from unwanted influences and toxic people.

I had wonderful co-workers and friends who supported me and provided help with physical duties I could not do on my own. But I yearned for support from other women who had experienced breast cancer who were proactive in their approach to cancer and who did not just blindly follow doctor's advice without doing research or critical thinking. People who had the desire to make the ultimate decisions about treatment and care took the time to find doctors who supported their decisions, and who had the ability to challenge standard-of-care approaches to treatment. I could not find that kind of supportive person where I lived. It is sorely lacking. It wasn't until a year after my surgery that I attended a free retreat for breast cancer survivors called Harmony Hill. It was only 3 days but it changed my life. It was what I was waiting for and what I need and the participants from my small group still communicate and support each other on a special, private face book page.

Mental health

I had done a year of EMDR therapy a few years before my diagnosis to deal with some trauma and anxiety in my life. My therapist was a breast cancer survivor, so she was one of the first people I called. We set up an appointment about two weeks after my surgery when I still had my drains. It was exhausting as I had to drive about one and one half hours plus take a ferry ride to get there, but it was worth it. It immediately helped me feel less anxious.

My co-workers and friends were wonderful but after the first month or so, since I seemed to look and feel okay, people stopped checking in with me. I really wanted to find other breast cancer survivors I could talk to. A big part of my healing comes from doing the things I love to do around people that are positive and nurturing, strong and like-minded.

I decided not to get reconstructive surgery early on. I think mostly due to my age, having breasts was not important to me. I figured if I was to start dating again, any man who was bothered by my lack of breasts was not the man for me. First, I had to deal with my feelings of revulsion when I looked at my chest in the mirror- all the scars, one "hump" being bigger than the other. I did research on what reconstruction entailed and talked to other breast cancer survivors about their thoughts on reconstruction and it confirmed for me that I did not want to get implants. Shopping has become so much fun as most tops fit better now.

I was also concerned that no reason was given for my disease. If I were given the predisposing factors for my disease, then I could work on reversing those factors in my life instead of just managing symptoms. I was given the option of chemotherapy. I did research on it and decided not to get it. My physician supported my decision. I checked in with her for the next couple of months and was supposed to get my six-month check-up in December, 2012. I waited until the end of December and had not heard from the doctor's office so I called and left a message for them to schedule my appointment. I never heard back.

A few months later, I heard from someone that my doctor had breast cancer herself and was planning to be back in June of 2013 to see clients. I went to her office to confirm this and asked that I be called in June to schedule my check-up. By August, I had heard nothing. My health insurance would out in one week. I could have gone to another doctor but it would have meant going off island. I continued seeing my naturopath instead to make sure my blood tests showed I was okay.

At first this really concerned me but as I continued to do research I realized this was for the best. I know my well-intentioned doctor, who is also a surgeon, would recommend taking tamoxifen and want to see me every six months. I knew I had to heal myself and not go the conventional route which only seemed to cause more problems than it solved.

I started right after my surgery to do everything I could do naturally to build up my immune system and cut down on inflammation in my body. I decided to treat risk factors to reverse, rather than just manage, the disease. I refused to be defined by the cancer and instead considered myself cancer-free. I wanted to treat the cause, not the symptoms. Traditional therapies seemed to treat the symptoms and not address the cause. Traditional health care has become heavily influenced by pharmacies, the big drug companies and managed care.

Re-framing my Disease

Statistics say that one in four die from cancer. I choose to think of it that three people of out four live. Why not be one of the three who live?

I finally have realized I am not immortal. I am only human. Cancer can happen to anyone and it happened to me. But even thought I am not sure what the future brings, I plan to make the time I choose to be as healthy and joyful as I can. I am not one of the people who say I had cancer and now that it is over, I am moving on. I am taking it as the wakeup call I needed to totally change my life in every aspect and remain mindful that if I go back to old habits, the cancer could come back. I choose to save my life right up until the end.

CHAPTER THREE

Re-entering the World
the Same but Different-
"But I Have Cancer!"

When I got home from surgery, I had about three weeks to recuperate enough to go back to work. I had lots of time to think and face the facts. I didn't want to go back to my life the way it was so I knew I had to make some major changes.

I had cancer. The surgery got it out, but there could still be cancer cells in my body. There is no cure for cancer, so I had to face the fact that I was left with managing a chronic disease. I had lived my life in denial up to this point and I knew I could no longer do that. I had a dog I adored, Spark, who needed me and that more than anything is what helped make my decision to live. To live as many years as I could, not knowing if I would die from cancer or something else, but to live a life of quality and not be defined by cancer.

As friends from work came by to leave food, do errands, walk my dog for me or just lift my spirits, I started talking to them about what I was thinking so I could voice my thoughts out loud. I would return to work and see how I did and then get my life back to normal the best I could. My humor kept me going and broke the ice when people came by not knowing what to say. I lifted up my top and showed the publisher of the newspaper I worked for my drains and said "this is how I am coming to work in two weeks!" She was startled at first then laughed so hard I thought she was going to crap her pants. I told my boss that if one of my drains popped out at work I may have to yell out, "Clean up on aisle five!"

A friend took me out for coffee at the drive-through and one of my drains did pop out. I made a joke about it: "Oh my God! What am I going to do if this happens with a stranger?" We both had a good laugh over that one.

I made the decision to stay on the island where I lived and ask my friends and co-workers for help, because I knew from experience that my own family could not handle what was happening with me. They would have made my recovery worse and set me back.

I came to the island looking for my community, but my community, mostly co-workers and clients, found me. It was a diverse group of people who were all kind and willing to help me. But I had to learn to ask for help, which is something I still am working on. I asked two co-workers to switch off days and come by after they got off work to check on me and lift things for me and take my dog for walks. When they didn't show up, I called them to remind them what they had promised. After that, they didn't miss a night and brought me food and whatever else I needed. They best part was just having company and someone to talk to.

This time of physical healing was also a time of deep reflection. What was my next step? Was my sales job too stressful for me to continue? If so, how could I get health insurance? Wasn't this the perfect time to write, which I had always wanted to do? Finally, I decided I would wait at least a year in my current job and pay off as much debt as I could, pay off my medical bills and make a plan for leaving my job. And that is exactly what I did. I quit my job one year and two weeks after my last surgery. I had paid off most of my debt, saved enough money to pay for COBRA so I could have medical coverage and pay my bills until my own business gave me enough money to survive. I started writing my book every day and joined a writers group. I started painting. I got food stamps and looked into getting catastrophic health insurance until I could get a better rate than COBRA through Obama Care in the next six months.

I came to realize we are all on unsure ground and we all must live with uncertainty to some degree. So I could learn to live with the uncertainty with more ease and joy and grace or I could choose to live in fear and anger. I needed to learn to release my grip on having certain outcomes in life and receive what was to come. I had to be vulnerable and allow my authentic self to be visible.

Seasons

We recognize and honor the seasons Answers come, small glimpses
Like the first tender shoots of grass
An idea, clue, hint
Of what we are about to learn as we go about the business of living our lives
Then we see it
The tiny shoot has become a full-grown blade of grass
Then a field of green
We recognize and honor all
The sadness and unwept tears we raced to avoid
Having traversed too fast over artificial ground
Our souls calls us back to ourselves
We are forced to slow down and face all the small miracles we missed along the way
The desire that drove us has died and we face a time of emptiness
There is nothing to do now but rest.

Writing to Heal

All my life I have danced around the written word, mostly as a reader. As a child, I spent many Saturdays at the public library carefully selecting my treasures for the week then waiting breathlessly while the librarian checked them out, relinquishing temporary custody to me. I always returned for more.

I wrote some stories in grade school for which my mother praised me. Later, I started a journal, which I continue to write in today. When odd thoughts, inspirations, prayers and phrases come to me, I throw them in a file called "personal."

The power of the written word has carried me through many losses and transitions. During my two divorces, bankruptcy and legal issues brought on from my second divorce, writing kept me sane. Added to that time was the revelation of my brother's alcoholism, a business failure, and the betrayal I faced from the man I thought had loved me. By writing about my feelings every day, I faced my own dark side and came out the other side, even though my family was not happy at being exposed. I'd be okay for a while and then I would have to face and endure another crisis in my life, mostly brought on by my family.

The year my dad got sick, I wrote in my journal as a way to face my pain as it came. When he died eight months later, I was able to be present enough to write a eulogy for him, which I read at his memorial service. This eulogy captured the essence of what was for me a life-long struggle with my dad. We were able to make peace with each other before he died. By voicing aloud the feelings I had on paper, I was able to start the grieving process. Many people came up to me after the service to thank me for my words and to tell me that they could relate to what I had shared from the heart and that they had similar situations in their own family.

Writing is how I heal and how I feel closer to the God of my understanding. It is when I can let go of control and let God minister to me. I am truly creative and my true artist self when I can forge a creative alliance, artist-to-artist, with God, the Great Creator. When I am in this place, I am willing to be in a place of uncertainty if it means I can write from my heart and be surprised by what is there.

Anxiety Soup

I hesitated to show my underachieving self
To anyone
Shame over my wounded family
Kept me stuck
I learned early on that as the
First born

I must step in and be the family hero
The fixer, the mediator and the controller I did my job so
well for so many years that
No one knew the truth.
Over a year ago, a crack appeared and
I collapsed under the weight of the entire pretense
The crack allowed in the air that saved my life.

Getting cancer re-awakened my desire to write. In fact, I got cancer, in part, because I had neglected my creativity for so many years and got caught up in the daily grind of life. It is a lesson I seem to need to relearn and surrender to over and over again in my life.

Birth Pains

I look over the landscape of my life
To see flattened bridges and roads full of potholes
The terrible times of suffering are the beginning of birth pains
And the promise of a new beginning
But the days of suffering have been too long and the labor
pains too intense.
Am I giving birth to a monster?
Or to a beautiful soul?

Where I have found myself stuck throughout my life is having these periods of creativity and realness then stopping myself when it got too scary. I would go back to believing that I was in control and let my ego rather than my heart (faith) guides me. Getting cancer turned things around for me and I had to admit I was not in control and that I needed to keep remembering that every day. I could not have a part-time, superficial belief in God, only trusting God when things got so bad I had no other choice. It had to be a full-time commitment. The only way I can call cancer a friend is to see that it is the only thing that brought me down to purgatory, which is where I needed to be to find paradise.

An old adage from early Grecian divers who hunted lobsters in the coral caves of the Aegean Islands speaks to me – "When swimming into a dark tunnel, there is a point of no return when you no longer have enough breath to double back. Your only choice is to swim forward into the unknown and pray for an exit." I had always allowed myself to only go so far, and then panic when the truth, darkness, and emotions got too close and real. Then I would scurry back to my safe life and think things were fine.

I had to listen to what this terrible disease was trying to tell me in order to save my life before it was too late. I had to stop putting others first and start taking care of myself.

Resurrected

I descend to the underworld as I rename myself as a woman.
At each of the seven gates,
I must strip myself of former trappings,
Until I stand naked.
I look for shortcuts until I realize
There are none.
I must give up the fight to make it all go away. I look in the
mirror and see a faint image
Of what I will be when I have been resurrected.

During my recovery work, I had a dream in which I was in a furniture store in the town where my parents lived. Several of the male sales clerks were going out of their way to disturb me by making a lot of noise and laughing at me. At some point I lost it and started hitting the men. The police were called. I felt that the policeman believed my part of the story and understood that I was acting out of character because I had been pushed beyond my limit. He followed me to my parent's house. Someone had already called to tell them what had happened, and I was relieved that I didn't have to tell them myself. I told my Dad that although I loved him, I could no longer carry his anger for him. He needed to take it back. The dream validated for me that the anger I held was not mine, and it was time to let it go.

This dream signaled the beginning of a profound way of being for me. I knew that the anger inside of me was partly due to the way I had been suppressed as a woman. It would change my way of being religious and spiritual, my relationships and the way I related to other women, men and myself.

I had to lose myself as a woman, or the old images of what a woman was, in order to create my new feminine self. This tied in directly to the loss of my breasts, which had defined, in part, what it meant to be a woman. The old images of being submissive, passive, sweet, and nice and a good daughter, wife, friend and employee no longer were working for me.

Unfamiliar Terrain

The horizon has changed and is overgrown
Old ideas, beliefs and ideals no longer fit.
A threshold is near.
My hand reaches out to an empty space
And touches the unknown

As I explored my new ideas of what it meant to be a woman, I began wondering why the church referred to God as male and why they routinely barred women, especially single women, from presiding over any important church roles. Why had I unconsciously agreed that a man is to be in charge and a woman's desires are to be secondary?

I had thought of myself as an independent woman. I was not outwardly submissive. I had a career, my own ideas and plans. I had traveled alone to Europe and Hawaii. I ate at restaurants and went to movies alone. But inside I was still caught up in daughterhood and was deferring to the father/male placed at the center. The truth was that my independence and outspokenness came at a great emotional cost and took a lot of energy. Without an authentic inner authority, and unable to access my feminine strength, I carried around a lot of fear of confrontation, criticism and of not pleasing.

As the cancer served to open my eyes and tear away my illusions, I was forced to see things I had not wanted to look at in the past. I could no longer live with a sense of false innocence. But once the blinders came off, there was no turning back. Like Gandhi, exploring injustice and no longer sustaining a punitive model of life that comes with patriarchy became my mission. This included the misconceptions I saw modeled in the health care industry.

Going Back to Work

As a busy career woman, I had no time for cancer. How dare this disease interrupt my busy life? I scheduled the surgery in my appointment book and did the tests my doctor told me to do and then went right back to work. Having cancer really did not fit into my schedule and I resented the hell out of the intrusion.

Being a very private person, I did not sign up to be a billboard for cancer. I did not want people feeling sorry for me or knowing the intimate details of my life and health. But maybe the drive that makes me successful in my career helped me fight the cancer and become a survivor.

I had to look at the role of stress in my life and wonder if this is what caused my cancer. I could have control over my work but I could not control my cancer and it scared me. I was uncertain. What would my future bring? Would I even be able to work again? Would I be able to take care of Spark? I was not sure if I would be able to keep my job, as I did not have enough vacation or sick time built up since I had been at it for less than a year. Would I even be physically able to return to work? I did not know what to expect.

Luckily, I worked for and with wonderful people at the time who allowed me to work part-time for a while. They also found a way to keep my job for me even though I received no pay for several months. I was also teaching online at the time, which provided some income.

I could laugh, cry and vent with my co-workers, but there was always the expectation that I needed to work hard and get the job done. I felt I needed to push myself to pull my weight those first few months back at work and I probably should have stayed home longer to recuperate. I just did not have enough paid time banked in order to do that.

My first day back at work was only three weeks after my second surgery and I still had my drains in my breasts. I thought I would be fine working a full day, but I got so tired and people told me I was looking extremely pale. So I went to my doctor and got a note saying I could only work part-time for the next month. That helped a lot. I learned to pace myself and not work so hard and not feel guilty about it. I did the best I could and started learning how to set better boundaries.

I told my doctor that I was worried about the stress involved in my sales job and that it would cause the cancer to come back. She told me I needed to do what made me happy. So I made a plan right then and there. I would stay at my job another year, pay off as much debt as I could, save some money and then quit. I needed to have the health insurance for one thing and I did not want to make another major change or life decision for a year.

I knew if I continued doing the same work, in the same way, I would set myself up for getting ill again. I had to make a drastic change. I just wasn't able to do it right away for financial reasons.

I was contacted by a friend who had found the perfect place for me to live but I could not face moving right after major surgery so I had to let it go. I ran into the owner of the home a few months later and she told me the place was still available. I set up a time to see the place a few days later and ended up signing a two year lease and moving the next month. Knowing my situation, my landlord and her family offered to move everything for me knowing my situation. All I did was get help packing up my stuff, pay for gas on the moving truck and handle all the moving details. It was the easiest move I have ever had and I love my house. I have a view from all my windows of the water and I am only a few blocks from the beach. It is a very healing, creative environment. Nature has always been a healing place for me so being so close to the water and beach has been a godsend for me.

The first person I contacted about my diagnosis was my boss as I had kept her up-to-date since my mammogram. She is a colon cancer survivor and was a wonderful resource for me during this time. We also laughed a lot as we share the same "sick" humor and made jokes about

Gail Rognan

cancer. One day she said, "Just think- this is the perfect time for you to run someone you don't like over in your car and just blame it on the cancer!" When I called with my diagnosis, she said "Oh, crap!" Then she let me know she was there for me. Several of my co-workers offered to give me their unused vacation time but I was told that our company did not allow this policy.

I could tell some people did not know what to say around me. So I used humor to break the ice and it helped me and others feel more comfortable. Even though I was such a private person, I chose to talk openly about my cancer journey, as I figured that was the best way to get support. It was also a way to help others going through the same thing. I had been working with an EMDR therapist those four months, and in my mind had transitioned from a victim to a survivor.

Getting Assistance

I got food stamps after quitting my job and felt no shame about it. I realize how far I have come because I am no longer willing or able to carry the burden of helping everyone else on my back. It was time for me to ask for help and to receive assistance I had paid for by working so many years.

I started seeing a local naturopath to monitor my health and added to the natural supplements I was taking to build up my immune system. I did check-ins with my doctor for 3 months. I waited for a call for my six month check in and never heard anything so I called the doctor's office and left a message to schedule an appointment. I never got a call back. Later, I heard from someone in the community that my doctor had breast cancer herself and was taking time off for her surgery and treatment. Because I no longer had health insurance, I was unable to go see her.

I did all I could with the resources I had to keep the cancer from coming back, which helped me feel at peace with my decision to follow an alternative health regimen. If I were to get cancer again, I would have to deal with what I would do at that time. After all the reading and research I have done since my diagnosis, I am not even sure if I would have surgery again and I already know I will never agree to chemotherapy or radiation because of all the side effects involved. Whatever comes my way, I trust myself to take the time to make the right decisions based on what I know and feel at the time.

Decision to Leave my Job

Work provided structure and normalcy for me. I needed to keep busy and not worry about whether the cancer would come back. But I also made a conscious choice to slow my pace of work and not kill myself to get the sale or meet my goal. I did not seek preferential treatment because of my illness, but I also let it be known I would not be taking on any extra work or staying longer hours. I took my hour lunch every day and took breaks throughout the day to rest for a few minutes.

The longer I stayed at my job, the more I could see that I could no longer pretend I was enthusiastic about it and I was no longer willing to give so much of myself for a job or company that gave so little back. There was incongruence between my core values of faith, integrity and creativity and what was asked for to be in advertising sales. I loved my clients and made quite a few friends, but I knew I had to create a simpler, less stressful life for myself. I had quit my job about four months before being diagnosed with cancer because I was tired and burned out from being expected to do so much because my co-workers either kept getting fired or quitting, leaving all the work for me. I was willing to step up temporarily but it kept happening over and over. They came back and gave me Mondays off and got me some help so I ended up staying another sixteen months.

One thing I became very conscious of was letting my co-workers know that I could not be exposed to sickness as my immune system was vulnerable. Many times my co-workers would come to work sick and I would politely ask them to stay away from me. I suggested they stay home when they were sick as it was putting my health at risk by exposing me to whatever they had. The workplace tends to reward people for working longer hours and putting their health at risk all in the name of profit. It takes a strong person to stand up to this and requires balance for the risk of appearing uncommitted to the company's bottom line.

I was able to change the way I viewed my work and authority figures during this time and do not regret the time I worked for this company. But when they said I needed to give up my Mondays about a year after giving them to me, I knew it was time to plan my departure. I was not willing to give up my life, health or well-being for any job.

I did a lot of praying and reflecting and budgeting to see if and when I could leave my job. I set a date to give my notice and decided I would start a pet sitting and dog walking business as I have always loved animals. I wanted to love and have fun with my work so I got a business license, liability insurance and business cards and started promoting myself. The day after I left my job, I was officially in business and slowly started getting jobs. Even though it was a crazy thing to do when the economy was still struggling, I knew I would be okay. I was willing to get a part-time job if necessary until my business could sustain me financially and I had quite a bit of savings to get me by for a while.

Suddenly I had the time to write daily and the means to pay my bills, while simplifying my life a good deal. Of course, I don't have a family to support- I just need to take care of myself and my new dog, Brodie.

My true self is a creative person, an artist, a leader, and a teacher. I believe that if we are not living being true to ourselves that we get sick. And that is what happened to me. I had always been afraid to come out as an artist because I believed what I had been told by my family and others about artists as being poor, lazy and flaky. I went back and forth all my life worrying about how I could be my creative self and still pay the bills.

The Rainbow Coat

In years past, there was a family of beavers who lived deep in the forest. They were a traditional family who did what was expected of them and the father's word was final in all things. But one of the beavers was different. She didn't see the purpose of always working to build dams in the streams and gnawing at wood. She tried hard to fit into her family and relatives but what she loved best was exploring in the woods and listening to the sounds of the forest, for here she felt that she could lean against the face of God.

Her family disapproved of her ways, especially her father who tried to rein her in by criticizing her free spirit ways and punishing her. Her family said things like – Why don't you act like a real beaver? You need to always be busy and accomplishing things instead of dreaming, writing and drawing. You are lazy and a flake. You need to be smiling all the time or people will think you are unhappy. Artists are crazy, broke, irresponsible, loners, doomed, unhappy, and born, not made.

This kind of talk would hurt and confuse little beaver. All she wanted to do was be herself and create. She wondered why she couldn't look and act like her family and friends. Wasn't it a wonderful thing to dream and to listen to the voice of God in the forest? No, her parents told her. It is not okay to dream or to be different. If you want to survive you must be busy all the time like us or you will die.

The family chaos and abuse was hidden behind their "perfect" family image and added to the little beaver's confusion about what was true. So she became very anxious and decided that she needed a coat to protect her from the outside chill. She created a "rainbow" coat of different colored bark and put it on. "I'll never be cold again," she told herself.

Her family admired her coat and the work it took to make it. They thought that it was a very sensible thing to do. She started working with her family without complaint and never had time to dream or create or talk to God anymore. Her coat became her "kick ass" self. It carried her buried rage and thought that the way to be safe was to be in control. She became very impatient with herself and others who didn't do things perfectly. She didn't want people to see her fear or sadness so she added more bark to her coat. At times, she became cruel and inconsistent and beat herself up when she was lazy.

She began to be angry at the injustice in the world but didn't know how to change it, and she became very career-orientated and hardly ever drew or wrote or prayed to her God, although there were times when she couldn't resist stopping and listening to the forest or the waves crashing on the shore in the distance. She would open up her coat (heart) a little to feel the breeze. Her heart would fill up with joy and then she would remember her father's words: to act like this made her a worthless beaver.

Gradually the beaver noticed that her coat was becoming heavier and heavier and parts of it were damaged. She kept adding new tree bark and leaves to patch it up. Then she would add flowers to decorate it a bit until it weighed her down to the point she could barely walk. She realized that she couldn't remember what her original fur looked like anymore.

"It has been so many years since I have let the breeze blow against my fur. I've loved this coat. It has protected me well. It has kept me warm, helped me accomplish things. But now it feels suffocating."

Her family and friends urged her to keep her coat on. They told her, "You will hurt us by going back to your old ways. Feelings have no place in this family. You will be alone. You will always be without money and struggle. You will get sick and die. You will never find a beaver to marry and have kids with. You are unworthy of success and love."

But with the coat on, the beaver could no longer swim or even do the work her family asked her to do. She so badly wanted to be free but she no longer knew how to remove the coat. She believed her family's words and not her own. She did remember that when she didn't wear the coat so very long ago, she felt lighter and free. She realized that just the opposite of what her family told her was true – if she kept the coat on she would get sick and die by suffocating to death.

Around this time, she befriended a wise owl. The owl urged her to take off the coat so she could play with him. He urged her to trust herself— although she may be uncomfortable and feel naked for a while without the coat, she wouldn't die.

The owl could see that the beaver was very strong and courageous and could protect herself without the coat. She could keep parts of the coat and use it when she needed it for motivation or extra armor. The owl convinced the beaver to remove the coat, one piece at a time. That way she could learn to feel again at her own pace.

The beaver found a safe place in the forest where she could remember who she was and where she could see, smell and hear the sounds of life and of God again. She began to remove pieces of her coat with the help of a few good friends. At first, she didn't recognize herself and felt out of sorts. But one, fine sunny day, she took off the last piece of bark. She slowly turned it over in her hands and thanked it for all that it had done for her She blessed it and put it in the stream of life, and swam free and unencumbered to find her destiny.

Because I have lived through many times of uncertainty and times of not knowing if I could pay my bills, I knew I would be okay this time. When I start panicking, when the stress of not knowing when the next check will come gets to me, I try and turn things around by asking myself, "How can I be of service today?" This helps me relax and put things in perspective. It is as if when I take my mind off my worries, the money has a space to fill and it just comes.

I took a class on practicing kindness to help myself become more conscious of being in service so it became a natural response for me. Before I had acted from "niceness" rather than "kindness" and there is a big difference. Niceness to me is false and meant stuffing my true feelings, which made my body pay the price. Kindness is speaking one's truth but in a respectful, gentle way.

But I knew that as much as the changes I was making were beneficial, it wasn't enough. I had to look deeply at the real reasons I got cancer. I needed to look back over my life and see where it went off track. I had to see when my light was extinguished.

CHAPTER FOUR

Looking at the Causes–
When the Light Went Out

Knowing Light

As a child, I knew the light
It lit me up from the inside and made my eyes shine
My warm heart
Was a beacon for weary travelers.
Years of struggle nearly extinguished the light
The weary traveler was I.
The embers heat up and will soon ignite
The years of chaos provide the kindling
My future self rises from the ashes.

We all need light to survive. In addition to raising our spirits, sunshine contributes to our physical health by providing Vitamin D. As spiritual beings, we also have a need for spiritual light. Many call this spiritual light "God" and this light serves to reveal the soul's path so we can find our way more easily in everyday life. When we are deprived of such light, we can easily lose ourselves to the distractions of the ego. But even in the darkness, God is there. It is us who move away from the light, not God who takes it from us.

As I look back on my life journey, I try to pinpoint exactly when my light was nearly extinguished. When did I began giving all the light I possessed away to others and none to myself? Louise Hay says that all disease comes from unforgiveness.[3] When it is problems involved with the breasts, it means a refusal to nourish the self, putting everyone else first, over mothering, overprotection and overbearing attitudes. Cancer is related to a deep hurt, longstanding resentment, a deep secret or grief eating away at the self. It is not what causes it, but may be what causes it to grow faster.

I had experienced many traumas throughout my life that re-opened the wound caused by the lack of love in childhood. Several experts say that one of the most common precursors of cancer is a traumatic loss or a feeling of emptiness in one's life. They say to look at what happened in the preceding months or years before the diagnosis of the illness. That it is not stress itself that causes cancer, but how we deal with stress. If our wounds have been improperly healed, then feelings of helplessness occur.

I had become complacent and almost a "recluse" when I worked from home for over six years as an online, adjunct college professor. I buried my emotions and pretended I was doing what I wanted as a career, but it was slowly killing my spirit and making my immune system weaker. A vigorous immune system can overcome cancer if it is not interfered with and emotional growth toward a greater self- acceptance and fulfillment helps keep it strong.

Because I did not grow up with the love I needed, I had to learn to love myself. I believe that all aspects of one's life, including mental health, must be healed in order to reverse the cancer process. It took over two years of a special kind of "body" therapy, known as EMDR, for me to learn how to do this.

Before I started doing the therapy and doing research, I was blaming myself for getting cancer. I learned that it takes four to forty years for normal cells to become abnormal cancer cells, and then a detectable tumor. During this process, cells that were initially healthy become seriously malfunctioning. This can be caused by abnormal genes, or much more commonly, exposure to radiation, environmental toxins

---

[3]   Louise L. Hay, *You Can Heal Your Life* (Carlsbad, CA: Hay House, 1999), 8.

or other carcinogens. Certain psychological states can profoundly influence the cancer cells to grow. Most cancer patients can tell of a period of major stress in the months or years before being diagnosed, such as feelings of helplessness, chronic conflict that seems will never be resolved or overwhelming obligations that create a feeling of suffocation. While these don't directly cause the cancer, they can give the cancer an opportunity to grow faster. Chronic stress affects our immune systems and throws our hormones out of balance.

The factors that can cause cancer are so numerous and varied there is no reason to blame ourselves or feel guilty for developing the disease. I believe that my personality was cancer-prone, as I never felt welcome in my childhood and received little encouragement for being my true, creative self. I compensated for this by conforming to what was expected of me: becoming a "nice" little girl who rarely showed anger or any emotion. I was always ready to help others and put others' needs before my own. I also overinvested in one single aspect of life- work. I became a workaholic and I identified myself by my work.

I had a difficult relationship with my Dad most of my life, until he died. I was angry at him for not loving me the way I needed to be loved. Instead, he seemed to criticize me all the time.

When the Light Went Out

It was the day after Christmas in 1997, and I received a call from my mom. She was crying as she told me that my dad was sick and in the hospital and that I needed to come as soon as possible. I had celebrated Christmas with my family the day before and I could tell that my father did not feel well. I remember having a premonition as I got in my car to go home that my parents would not be alive forever. Heaviness descended on me and I shook it off.

I got to the hospital as soon as I could. My mom was acting as if it was nothing serious but I could sense that things were terribly wrong. The thought that my father could die terrified me, not only because I loved him more than anyone, but also because he and I had so much unfinished business. We'd had a falling out just before Christmas. I had written him a letter expressing my frustration at being constantly criticized by him, never being and doing enough and did not want to be around him that Christmas. My mom talked me into coming and I am glad she did.

When he got sick, I felt terribly guilty, like I had caused his illness. I should have swallowed my words and pretended that everything was okay between us. But here he was, close to death, and I decided this was the time I could make peace with him. I no longer wanted to keep him at arm's length but be closer to him and remember what it was that I loved about him. I would be responsible for what I brought to our visits and be authentic. It was as if God were saying to me "Ok, it is time to be a grown-up now."

A Light at the End of the Tunnel

My father was drugged up and seemed not to know me as he lay hooked up to monitors in intensive care. Normally a tall, heavy-set, imposing man, he looked pale and shrunken lying in the bed at the hospital. He was diagnosed with acute pancreatitis, an inflammation of the pancreas caused by problems with gallstones, which most people don't survive. My father, a proud and stubborn man, fought back and survived. I am so grateful that he passed on those qualities to me as I would need them later when I was diagnosed with cancer.

As I stood by his bed, I felt lost. After years of loving my father from a safe distance, I felt confused being so close to him and seeing him so vulnerable. At almost forty years old, I still could not stand in his presence as a grown woman. I felt like a little girl again, eager to please and still fearful of his disapproval.

Growing up, I had learned the power of words to either lift up or destroy. I learned to keep quiet. When I did speak up he would counter with "can't you take a joke?" I learned to settle for rolling my eyes and walking away in silence. Slowly, over the years, my light became dimmer.

As I held my dad's hand as I sat next to his hospital bed, tears welled up in his eyes and he squeezed my hand. Even doing this was a big risk for me, as showing affection was not our normal way of interacting with each other. I had blamed him for our lack of closeness, but knowing he may die, I had to look at my own part in our alienation. My attempts at being closer to him were also for my own benefit.

I wanted to say to him "Daddy, I have always loved you. Do you know that? Why were you mad at me so much? Are you proud of me?"

Even though I was unable to say the words aloud, my Dad and I made our peace before he died about six months later. Later, I found out how much this peace between us meant to my dad when I had a session with a "medium" and my Dad's spirit came through and told me all the things I had waited to hear from him all of my life.

A Time of Spiritual Darkness

I needed to look back even further to see when my spiritual light began to be extinguished. It began in childhood. My relationship with God was always my beacon since I can remember. But because of the dysfunctional environment I grew up in, my images of God began to be distorted As nearly as I can tell, the repression of my spiritual light began when I was around eight or nine years old. I did not get the love or protection I needed and I believed God was not providing me with the love and protection I needed either. I became hurt and angry and slowly closed myself off. I started keeping my distance from God. I put most of my love towards the family pets as I love animals and still do to this day. I made a decision I would go it alone.

Even though I got away to my grandparent's resort or friend's houses, my issues followed me. When I went away to college which was about an hour from home, I fell in love with creative writing and literature and majored in English. In retrospect, this was my desire for closeness with God re-surfacing, as a search for beauty and truth in the written word.

I struggled with how to be a person of strong faith in the workplace and at graduate school. I continued to keep quiet about my beliefs for fear of being criticized or judged. I did do my thesis on "spirituality in the workplace" as a way to help myself figure out how to be in the world.

To compensate for my increasing uncomfortableness, I started eating as a way to stuff my feelings.

I searched for light in different people and experiences; in a human potential training, in different churches, in many different relationships. The men I dated were often elusive and even unkind to me. I tried to find the light in many different jobs. Many losses, betrayals, disappointments and abuse took more and more of my light away.

A Dark Tunnel

About seventeen years before I was diagnosed with cancer, I ended up losing everything because of my second marriage: the ad agency I ran, my good credit, my hopes and dreams that I could ever have a happy marriage and family of my own. I had no energy to work. I went through a major depression. For the first time in my life, I could not pull myself back up. The only way I got through the day was to read the bible, pray, walk and write. I had a friend who would call me every day and tell me that God had a plan for me and to not give up. I slowly started to feel that maybe I wasn't alone and God was someone who I could count on again.

I forced myself to become extroverted to gain approval, when my true self was an introvert. When you act from false motivations, you become exhausted and depleted, afraid that you will be rejected. My true self is a bit crazy, childlike, brilliant, extremely creative and caring.

All the negative emotions and toxic relationships in my life needed to be healed. Every trauma, loss, stress that was not resolved affected the health of my cells. The situation or trauma themselves did not cause the cancer, but the absence of love, the unresolved grief and pain led to the cancer process. It weakened my immune system and the cancer cells already there were provided with the fertile ground to grow.

My Dark Night of the Soul

In 2009, three years before my diagnosis, I had an experience with a person who lived below me in an apartment complex. He was upset by me walking around in my apartment and it made me feel very anxious.

Luckily, I had someone in my life who I talked to every week who knew me well: my spiritual director of seven years. She could tell something was very wrong. I was overreacting to something that was triggering a past trauma I had not dealt with. I was having an anxiety attack. I had become disconnected to what was Holy to me. I believed that God was not there for me.

It was exhausting to be on guard and hyper vigilant at all times. I had to admit to myself that I had been doing this for a long time while wearing a mask indicating things were peachy in my life. I realized my fear was irrational. So I talked to my spiritual director about it and she recommended that I get some help with my anxiety. That was what led me to finding my EMDR therapist, which helped save my life. I was able to explore the fear and see what was really behind it. This fear had ruled my life for too long.

I had spent most of my adult life believing I could protect myself and prevent something terrible from happening to me. That I could somehow prevent pain and suffering. I falsely believed that I was in control and I was alone in carrying myself through the storms.

The truth is I was never alone. The foundation of my life was being shaken and it was God who was shaking it to get my attention. The truth was I was never in control. I was always surrounded by God and the angels and all those who love me.

My real fear was being separated from my one source of love-God. I needed to come home to my body in a safe place without judgment and find my voice. I now commit daily to never losing this connection to God again and to remind myself that I am not in control and must surrender to God.

Medical Causes

I believe the tumor grew in me because of an imbalance in my body/hormones and I needed to reverse that process by mind, body and spirit practices that heal the whole person, not just the tumor. When we feel empowered, the immune system is empowered.

From my research, I learned from Francis that there is only one disease but it manifests in different ways and with different symptoms in different people. There is also one treatment of the one disease which is restoring cells to normal function, which eliminates all symptoms. Either the cells are getting too little or too much of what they need-deficiency or toxicity.

Francis explains that George C. Pack, a cancer specialist at Cornell Medical School, discovered that the only real defense against cancer is the immune system.[4] We all produce cancer every day, but if our immune system is where it needs to be, we will fight off the cancer cells. He explained that once a person has developed cancer, even though treatments may get it in remission, it will likely occur again unless the body conditions that allowed it to develop in the first place are reversed.

Cancer is a biological process, not a thing. Certain conditions are required for the process to operate and tumors are the products of this process, not symptoms. So what needs to be addressed is the process, not the tumor itself. To win, you need to shut down the process, not kill the tumor. Conventional therapies suppress the symptoms while weakening the immune system which contributes to the cancer process. The cancer comes back, usually worse than before. I did research on alternative treatments that would help strengthen my immune system; this led me to vitamin C IV's which I was able to get at my local naturopath. But I also had to replace the deficiencies in my organs and balance my hormones which I continue to do. It is a complex and lengthy process which I feel is necessary to becoming well.

Francis tells how German chemist Otto Warburg discovered in 1910 that cancer is caused by lack of oxygen respiration in the cells and replacement by sugar fermentation that creates energy (the kind of energy that does not serve the body).[5] Cancer cells produce energy by fermenting sugar in the absence of oxygen. Deemed too simple by the medical establishment, this discovery if publicized and used as standard

---

[4] Raymond M. Francis, MSC, *Never Fear Cancer Again: How to prevent and reverse cancer* (Deerfield, FL, Health Communications, 2011), 63-65.

[5] Raymond M. Francis, MSC, *Never Fear Cancer Again: How to prevent and reverse cancer* (Deerfield, FL, Health Communications, 2011), 63-65.

protocol, could endanger the entire cancer industry which depends on the money from conventional treatments given to eighty percent of cancer patients. Warburg believed increasing the amount of oxygen in the cancer cell will kill the cell. In my research, I came across something called food-grade hydrogen peroxide. It provides oxygen to the body. I read everything I could find on it and found a safe program to follow and started drinking drops of it in pure water daily. It serves to kill the cancer cells as they do not like oxygen. I know many people will disagree with this unorthodox treatment, but I truly believe it is helping to make my cells healthy. Increasing the amount of oxygen in the cell will kill the cancer cell.

My Self-Healing Diagnosis

I started formulating my personal healing plan. I knew that I needed to find my local tribe of like-minded, spiritual, creative people who have healed themselves and become whole and are doing what they can to heal the world. Sometimes I still feel lonely and I tend to be a "home-body." I need to be social and be around people, even if it means writing at the coffee shop every day. I put a posting in a local online social media site asking for my "tribe" to contact me and within a month, my group had formed. It is the community I have searched for all my life. I took a risk and asked for what I needed- intimacy- and that is what I received.

I made a commitment to stick to my resolve to never come back to the sales job I had at the newspaper. I resolved to keep asking my body what it needs to heal, to love out my purpose and to have more balance in my life. I knew I needed to open myself up the possibility of having a healthy sex life with no breasts! I needed to heal emotionally from the scars from my mastectomy. I needed to continue to refine my diet and lose at least 25 more lbs. and stay under 200 lbs. for the rest of my life. I needed to finish writing my book and get it published to aid in my healing and help others heal I needed to keep teaching but in a healthy way, as a spiritual practice. I needed to be part of the change in the health care system- a change agent or health care revolutionary to help bring the care back to health care. I needed to relax more. There is scientific proof that eliciting relaxation responses induces positive hormonal changes and returns the body to its natural state of homoeostasis which can induce self-repair of the body. I needed to understand the relationship between the mind, body and spirit so I could heal each of these in order to become whole and healthy.

But most of all, I needed to understand the connection between my mind, body and spirit, so I could begin the process of healing on all levels.

Chapter Five

Healing My Mind

Revisiting Trauma

This is the season of my harvest
When past pain surfaces to take me
Where I don't want to go.
Twisted branches long to be disentangled from my heart.
For too long, my sight was darkened
When I should have felt safe enough to leap into love.
My sight focuses on mourning
As I ready myself to see everything that has
Waited all these years for my return.
I am blessed with compassionate guides,
As I scrape away layers
For the first time, I am reunited with my banished heart
Now healed.
I feel the buoyant, clear air caress my newness.

Being on the verge of death makes you vulnerable. You learn quickly to immediately incorporate the lessons you needed to learn. I could no longer pretend that I would live forever. But I did have a choice of whether I wanted to heal the self of which cancer was only a small part. You feel so alone and you don't know where to turn. Because I went against conventional wisdom, and chose to heal myself with alternative treatment, this only increased my sense of aloneness. It all came down to me and God, and this is what finally led me to give my life over totally to God. I believe that God led me to the therapies that were right for me. I believe that He/She put them in my path for me to discover. If

God wanted me to live, I would live no matter what treatment I ended up using as long as I took the steps to become well and I had a desire to live. I also believe that if it was my time to pass over or ascend to the other side (for me, this is Heaven) then that is what would happen, no matter what I did to treat myself. But I made a choice to live well and make myself healthy, to resolve my emotional issues, and to resolve any karma left unresolved, no matter what time I had left on earth. I learned from my friend Janice that in order to die well, I had to learn to live well.

So when my doctor herself got breast cancer and was unavailable for check-ups, it was terrifying for me at first. But it forced me to do what I could do to make myself better while I waited for her to get better and return to her job. But once I started doing the research and prayed about what was right for me, I am so glad things happened the way they did. I no longer had health insurance, so I could not afford to see her or get any conventional treatments. But even if I could, I would not get them now. I know too much now to go back and pretend. This time on my own has forced me to go deep inside and learn to heal myself.

I started to educate myself and read everything I could on cancer and what causes it and about alternative health treatments. This helped take the fear of dying away as I learned that cancer is reversible if you are willing to detoxify your body and feed it with proper nutrition. It empowered me. I figured if I was to die from cancer, then it would be on my terms. I would refuse to live a life of putting poison in my body, taking toxic drugs with terrible side effects, spending my days in doctors' offices and in hospitals, always waiting for the next test to see if I was cancer-free, waiting to see if I could move on with my life. But this is something I had to make a decision about several times. When I would get scared that I wasn't doing enough, I would doubt myself. It is by re-reading my own book as I wrote it that kept me on my path.

Having cancer taught me that I had to learn to take care of myself, really love and adore myself enough to do whatever it took to bring myself back to my senses and make myself more mindful. Writing this book has been a good way to do this. It keeps me close to the truth and reminds me not to get lazy and go back to my old habits. Becoming more mindful includes all three areas of my life- body, mind and spirit, which I see now as inseparable.

I believe that we need to take a comprehensive approach to defeating cancer to make sure all of the potential causes are being addressed.

1. Nutrition – cut out processed food, sugar, etc.
2. Toxins – the need for detox; I do cleanses of all organs in my body twice a year
3. Mental- every thought has a biological consequence
4. Physical – need to move and stretch, protect self from X-rays (radiation), get sunlight and get enough sleep
5. Genetic- need to protect against damage to our genes
6. Medical – use alternative care (God given, natural foods and supplements) for chronic disease
7. Spiritual- getting self right with God

I believe this is a life-long approach. If we revert back to our old, unhealthy ways, the cancer will likely come back. We must educate our minds on what we need to do to reverse the cancer process and become well.

Cancer is not a thing. It is a biological process that requires certain conditions for the process to operate. Tumors are products of this process- not symptoms. Cancer is not the tumor. Cancer is the process that created the tumor. By the time it is diagnosed, you've had it for years or even decades. What needs to be addressed is the process that produced the tumor, not the tumor itself. To win, you have to shut down the process, not kill the tumor. Conventional therapies only serve to suppress the symptoms while weakening the immune system which contributes to the cancer process. The cancer can come back, even worse than before.

Mind

"Every day, in every way, I am getting better and better."

The first step I needed to take was believing this and knowing I wanted to live. The mind's role in curing disease has not been proven scientifically, but millions attest to the power of a positive attitude and emotions to becoming well. We can purposefully cultivate and strengthen our will to live. I decided I would rather be out enjoying nature than sitting alone in my house or in a doctor's office, depressed and angry, withdrawing from the world.

I decided to live with hope and the expectation that I would be healthy.

I had no model of how to love myself so I had to relearn how to do this in my therapy. I had to change my mind about how I felt about myself because the mind directly affects our health. The extent that we love ourselves determines whether we eat right; get enough sleep, exercise and much more.

The mind acts directly on the body's tissues which respond to the mind's live or die messages. Cancer appears when the immune system becomes suppressed and can no longer deal with the constant requirement of the white blood cells fending off attacks on our bodies. (Stress response). Passive emotions, such as the suppression of anger, also suppress the immune system. We can change how DNA expresses itself by utilizing the power of our mind. Thoughts about our health stem from childhood, when negative thoughts about our health may have been programmed.

If you take sick cells out of the bad environment, they totally recover without medicine. It is all in how the mind interprets an event. The body can be changed by dealing with how we feel. The point to get to is to know that life is difficult but also desirable.

Radical forgiveness

Stored impressions, memories can start up and run endlessly throughout life. This mindless repetition continues unless we shine a light of awareness on them and delete the old programs and lay down new mental tracks. Unless we do this, we believe and act on opinions and assumptions as if they are reality, shutting out new possibilities. If things get stuck in our mind (bodies), we become unbalanced physically, emotionally and spiritually.

Things aren't always what they seem. What appears to be unfair and cruel (like getting cancer!) may be what we called forth and is exactly what we needed. It could be the key to our healing something that has blocked us from being happy or growing. I believe that is what happened for me.

I have felt for some time that we are all being called to move quicker through our lessons in preparation for a profound shift of some kind in the world. But that can be scary. It took me getting cancer to finally agree to do my part regardless of the consequences.

The earth has a cancer: the human race. We have stepped out of the natural balance of things and have come to believe that we can control and dominate the entire system. Just as toxic drugs and other violent treatments will not cure cancer, violent, high-tech solutions to the earth's problems won't work either.

My mission became to come back to this lifetime as a survivor of cancer in order to demonstrate the futility of projecting anger and war on the body and on ourselves. The mission is to help us all understand that *love* is the only answer. But, first, I had to learn to love myself and receive the love that others offered. I believe that cancer was what it took for me to finally see how much I was loved and to finally allow myself to receive that love.

For me to change my negative stored impressions, I had to get intensive therapy called EMDR- Eye Movement Desensitization Reprocessing. I had done talk therapy in the past but it only helped for a while, then I would move back into old patterns. I needed to address the trauma stored in my body, deposited from numerous traumatic experiences in my life that I had not fully dealt with. EMDR allows changes to occur within weeks, whereas other forms of therapy can take years. EMDR places the information processing system of the brain first in the treatment of pathology. Disturbing events are revisited and appropriate brain connections are made that return us to emotional equilibrium. When a memory is too disturbing it overwhelms the information processing system and gets stored in the body's memory, along with unpleasant emotions, physical sensations and beliefs. I would come to a session with anxiety and allow myself to surrender to the process and my right brain would take over. Pains I had when starting the sessions would disappear and I would leave feeling a totally different way about the experience I dealt with in that session. It took away self-blame, guilt and anger and replaced them with empowerment, peace and self-love.

The immune system is controlled by the brain and indirectly through the hormones in the bloodstream. Cancer appears when the immune system becomes suppressed and can no longer deal with the routine threat of the cancer cells in everyone's bodies which normally are destroyed by our white blood cells before they turn into tumors.

Chronic stress causes hormones released by the adrenal gland to suppress the immune system. Also, passive emotions such as feelings of failure and suppression of anger produce the same hormones which suppress the immune system.

Our state of mind has an immediate and direct effect on our bodies. For example, if we ignore feelings of despair, our body receives a message to "die." If we seek help for our feelings of despair we can turn things around and realize that even though life is difficult, it is still desirable. EMDR helps our bodies and minds to communicate with each other by changing emotions and imagery.

So when I was diagnosed for a second time with cancer two years after the first diagnosis, I was able to react in a new way after all my work on myself. Since I was sure I would die of cancer at some point, I decided this was the worst thing that could happen to me. I decided there were two options to deal with this- either go around feeling miserable and angry and waste what life I did have, or live life to the fullest every day. Because I am a fighter, I chose the latter. Whether I was right or wrong in my theories, I took on the fight wholeheartedly. Then, without realizing it, I just may turn into one of the exceptions. One of the people who go on to live many years.

When we suffer an emotional loss and don't properly deal with it, the body often responds by developing a new growth (tumor).

Radical Love

Today I got a healing treatment
From someone I trust deeply
The tight spot in my back
When touched
Made me cry out,
Releasing old memories and feelings
In the spot where I hold out love
Hold out God.
So tight, so hunched over, so curled in
That rigamortis had almost set in
The touch gave me a glimpse
A long flash
Of what it is like to feel God's love all the time.

The Effects of Stress and Depression

Too much stress that is not handled well can lead to depression. Depression affects the immune system and this can be manifested very quickly if some remnant of a previous disease remains. Despair depresses our immune system, allowing residual cancer cells that were under control to multiply again. So my main goal now is to do everything I can possibly do to stay well in all ways and deal with the unavoidable emotional problems in my life as they come up. Over time, the negative beliefs that repetitively trigger the stress response take their toll. The cellular environment gets poisoned with the stress hormones.

Our beliefs manifest physically. If a doctor tells you that cancer is a chronic disease that must be managed the rest of your life, it sets you up to believe that and feel you will never be well. This activates the stress response. If we believe we are cancer-free and that we will be well, we will be well.

When I would have EMDR or acupuncture treatments, I believed that they would work, so they did. The therapy and treatments were also done by great healers.

53

Every day I would make the choice to not give up or quit. Every day I made the decision to live. To not lose interest in life, work, people, hobbies, and in my dreams.

Because I have been programmed by my family to put others' needs before my own and be a "good girl," I had to learn to put myself first. Getting cancer was what re-directed my life and made me well today because I was no longer willing to live the old way.

The Effects of Humor and Laughter

Humor, not something that probably comes to mind with cancer, has positive effects in making a disease easier to bear. It boosts our mood, helps us relax, reduces stress and improves our quality of life. It can help deal with pain and give an increased sense of well-being. I don't know if there is scientific proof that it builds your immune system, but I believe that it does. I know it helped people around me relax when they didn't know what to say. It helped them see I could laugh about it so they could joke. The journey would have been much worse for me without humor as I have always used it to get through tough situations.

Some days I would come into work determined to be depressed and my boss would see me walk by her office and call me in. She would say something totally outrageous and it would get me out of my mood. We would get to laughing so hard, I'd have to run to the bathroom to avoid crapping my pants. She would say something like, "Just think, this is the perfect time to run someone you don't like down in your car. You can get out of your car and say, "Sorry, I have cancer!"

Humor contains an element of surprise. A joke's punch line and skewed logic can short-circuit the cerebral brain. There is also an element of suffering at the core of humor. Disease happens when the mind, body and spirit are out of balance.

The world can be seen as having a cancer—the human race—which is destroying civilization as we know it. I believe that our salvation lies in remembering the truth of who we are. We are God's creation. We must be in touch with God's spirit at all times and not allow ourselves to become separated from our source.

CHAPTER SIX

Healing my Body

When words can't be expressed
On paper, or out loud
My body speaks for me.
The hunger and desire in my body
Propels me in directions not fully understood
Filling me with feelings yet unexpressed
I long to get to the center of my body
To the center of myself, my holy place
And to live there forever.

We deposit our misery, our unexpressed feeling somewhere in our body. Louise Hay, in *Heal Your Body*, connects body issues and illnesses with their underlying emotional dysfunction. My body's message to me was that I needed to heal the deep wounds I had and become more whole. That I needed to express myself, my creativity and let my energy flow. If I chose to not do this, then I'd better be beware of the consequences! If we don't respond to the first gentle nudges our body gives us, they will increase in intensity.

Doing the work in EMDR and somatic therapy helped me deal with these issues. I lost over sixty pounds and kept forty of it off. I am working on losing thirty more pounds. My adrenal, thyroid and blood pressure are all normal. I am still working on cleansing my liver and it is working. Not only am I using supplements my naturopath sent me but I am more mindful of when I complain and feel bad and make a switch so I feel more positive.

I started to see my body as my companion, to be loved and heard, as it had messages to give me. My aches and pains became my "angels," bringing me warnings of unfaced stress I needed to pay attention to. I began to believe that God could do transforming work right there in my body if I allowed it. I had to face some hard-to-face truths. My basic need for love was not met in my family. But instead of letting God fill the void, I tried to find it in all the wrong places.

Body Talk

My story lies deep in my body's memory,
Protected by layers of fat.
Bits of it surge to the forefront, unexpectantly giving me glimpses of my long-lost self,
And the all-knowing one, who longs to embrace, bless and heal all of me
My story can't be figured out.
It speaks to me in its own time, and on its own terms
As I stay connected to my feeling
My body reveals clues and chapters.

I needed to slow down and nurture my body, to redirect my energy and choose leisure over work, to figure out why I am so impatient so I could relax. I was no longer willing to violate my body by eating to fill emptiness. I needed to face feelings I had tried to push down with food before. I literally needed to get things off my chest!

What it all comes down to is I finally stopped to listen to the wake-up calls I had ignored before and come to my senses in all areas of my life so I could stay balanced and mindful. This is what cancer did for me- it woke me up. I know now that if I forget what can happen and go back to my old ways, I could get cancer again. I am unwilling to do that. In the face of death, I found the strength to forgive myself for violating my body and for being mindless. I found deep energy, deep breathing and meditation to give me the strength, stretching and stillness I needed to heal.

Bernie Siegel says that right down to the cellular level, our bodies know what we are to become.[6] The body is a channel to the soul. Rather than using the illness to beat ourselves up, or set off on a crusade to figure out why bad things happen to good people, we can use the illness to get our attention.

My body has a deep desire to live. It has an incredible tolerance for damage and destruction. I believe that we live as long as our soul needs our bodies. We live as long as we do because of the care we give to our bodies. The care we give to our bodies determines the quality of life we will have, but not the length of life.

Getting ill also woke me up to my body and made me pay attention to it. Siegel writes, "Diseases can be our spiritual flat tires- disruptions in our lives that seem to be disastrous at the time but end by re-directing our lives in a meaningful way."[6] I could no longer view my body as a machine to be driven and manipulated. Now I needed to see it as my companion who needed to be loved and listened to, a sanctuary to be worshipped.

Harboring toxic emotions and suppressing feelings affects one's body. Holding trauma in the body's tissues causes toxins to build up which can lead to disease.

I started asking my body what it needed to tell me. One day, I wrote a letter as if my cancer were talking to me.

Dear Gail,

I am your cancer. I know you hate me and worry that I will come back. But I came to you to get you to listen and to wake up. I have done that and I won't be coming back unless you revert back to your old, negative habits. You have put everyone before yourself. Now you are cutting the negative, toxic draining people and situations out of your life and setting better boundaries. You are learning to love and take care of yourself.

---

[6] Bernie S. Siegel, M.D., *Love, Medicine & Miracles* (Novato, CA, New World Communications, 1998), 6.

Your double mastectomy saved your life because it gave you the peace of mind to relax enough to do the thinking and research needed to find your right path of healing.

I made you better and stronger and now you understand that you can never live your life like you were. You need to make your body strong and healthy so the cancer cells still left in your body will not grow into another tumor.

The natural way you are healing your body is killing me. I can't live without what feeds me. You have figured that out and are winning the war. Your strong faith in God is your biggest protection and blessing.

Consider me a blessing and not a monster.

Signed,
Your cancer

Body Therapy

EMDR and Somatic therapy work by healing trauma that is within our body and needs to be brought out in the open and healed. In this type of therapy, I found a safe place to face some hard truths I had resisted facing in the past. Working with my acupuncturist also helped me release emotions that were stuck in my body which, in turn, released the swelling in my breasts after my surgery. I could visualize my breasts healing as I let go of past hurts and loss.

EMDR stands for Eye Movement Desensitization and Reprocessing and works with patients who have experienced PSTD (posttraumatic stress disorder). The process works much faster and more effectively than talk therapy, as it works with the brain to restore emotional equilibrium. It takes disturbing events and makes the brain make the connections that are appropriate to make negative reactions disappear.

Extremely disturbing events (i.e. getting a cancer diagnosis) can overwhelm the information-processing system and the negative experience is stored in the memory along with unpleasant emotions, physical sensations and beliefs. EMDR identifies the earlier life experiences that trigger unpleasant memories, and are the basis of current problems. The earlier memories are accessed which activates the brain's information-processing system by use of the bilateral eye movements, taps or tones. What is useful is incorporated and what is useless is discarded, leaving the patient feeling empowered. Even general life events can cause major trauma.

Somatic Therapy

Along with EMDR therapy, I received somatic therapy. Somatic therapy is a holistically oriented therapy which integrates our mental, emotional, spiritual and physical aspects. It accomplishes this by helping us to become aware of the sensations we experience in our bodies. When our mind becomes focused on worries, schedules and concerns, our body's awareness and breathing can help us shift our focus to what we are experiencing in the moment. When we take the time to focus, we can become aware of those places where we are "holding." That is, we can recognize those places where we are tight, sore or uncomfortable, whether it be our stomach, shoulders, neck or head.

Those areas where we are tight are areas where we are somehow holding on to something. Whenever we have had some painful or traumatic experience, we carry not only the memory and feelings connected with that experience, but we remember it physically as well. It is a kind of bodily memory of that event. And it is expressed through a contraction of muscle or of tissue or a loss of freely flowing energy in an area of our body that is in some way connected with that event for us. Sometimes that connection may be very symbolic. Perhaps we struggle with someone who is a real pain in the neck and we find that our neck becomes tight when we are around them. Many times we may not be aware of what the connection is. It is not nearly as important to understand what the connection is as it is to simply be aware of what we are experiencing.

It may seem strange to include therapy in a chapter about healing the body, but EMDR and somatic therapy are primarily a way of healing trauma in our body, which also heals our mind and spirit in the process. Since the memories are stored in our bodies, EMDR and somatic therapies are much shorter therapies but do not skip any of the stages of mourning. The memories are digested, or "metabolized," and lose their capacity to set off debilitating emotions. We can look back on the memory as an observer of simply a memory, stripped of its emotional charge. This process is what allowed me to rediscover my inner strength, confront my disease, as well as the prospect of death, with calm and greater serenity.

People would comment on this serenity that seemed to radiate from me. So even though the therapy did not cure me of cancer, it helped cure the feelings of helplessness I had and moved me from feeling like a victim to a survivor.

I also worked with a skilled acupuncturist for many years to increase my body awareness and healing. My acupuncturist was also trained in shamanistic healing and used a technique using rattles with me numerous times. As soon as the rattles started, we would both go into a trance state and I would start seeing visions. One time I saw a flying fish come sideways out of my body and saw the word "marlin" in my mind. When I looked up the symbolic meaning of "marlin" later, I found that it symbolizes the power of being alone with confidence and having an inward peaceful strength. The marlin teaches sensitivity in the emotional realms and changing pressures of daily life. Also, the power of words and the important role they play in communicating with tact and how to be powerful and use emotional acrobatics when necessary. All things I needed to learn.

In the Fisher King myths, the hero in the story finds a sacred fish. The visionary moment comes from beneath the sea, or the depths of the consciousness, to transform our lives. Coming from a Christian perspective, these moments connect us with the divine.

After the vision, I asked my healer if she had seen anything, without telling her what I had seen. She said she saw an object fly out on my body. Shamanism is a primitive, religious system where a medicine man or woman relies on their spiritual powers, or mind-body healing to heal.

The gods and spirits work through the shaman to heal the person. The spirit battle needs to be won over the evil spirits.

God's Laws

To stay healthy, we must obey nature's laws. We get off track when we eat junk food, live in toxic environments, don't exercise, live high-stress lifestyles and have exposure to artificial light. The immune system becomes overworked and depleted. I was led to a book that explained how, if we return to food as God created it, we will return to health. This includes animal protein, but it must be grass-fed and organic. We have two brains in our body: the one in our head and the other is in our gut. The healing of the digestive system positively affects the immune system, endocrine system, heart, lungs, blood supply, brain and the total nervous system. Thirty to sixty percent of all our calories need to come from fruits and vegetables. It says to eat whole grains that have been soaked, sprouted or fermented.

To turn things around, we must change our internal environment to one which supports our health. We must give our cells the nutrients they need and reduce the toxic load to live a lifestyle that supports health, not disease.

Cancer is not confined to one part of the body. It is everywhere. It is a systemic disease- a whole body problem. It is not a thing you can just cut out, poison or burn. It is a biological process that affects the entire body. There is only one cancer no matter what part of the body is involved. There is only one disease: malfunctioning cells.

With one-half of all Americans expected to get cancer in their lifetime, the cancer industry is huge and growing and very profitable. But conventional treatments don't work because cancer is a biological process. The tumor is the symptom, a product of the cancer process, and yet the cancer industry puts all the attention on the symptom and not the process.

When a new tumor began growing on my right chest again about two years after my mascetomony, I had educated myself on this process, and immediately started getting vitamin C IV'S, did an extensive cleanse process of all my organs- colon, candida/ parasite, kidney and liver. I started getting reiki healings done which is an energy healing therapy, and along with that, I am visualizing my body as completely balanced and completely healed.

I know now that cancer is not my enemy but a messenger sent to me to change my ways. It has led me to learn how to heal myself. I am not as afraid of cancer and can now see any manifestation of it as my body telling me I still have things to learn and heal.

CHAPTER SEVEN

Healing My Spirit - A Shift Takes Place

It takes an extraordinary confluence of events for us to become ill and then find our way home to good health. For me, it took two divorces, bankruptcy, my father's illness and death, a failing business, a business partner threatening to sue me, and getting cancer for me to finally wake up. The moment a person learns they have a chronic, serious disease, a profound shift takes place. We become aware of what really matters. For me, it was building better relationships with family and friends, finding a like-minded community, getting my health back and giving my life over totally to God.

My belief is that we have an absolute need for a spiritual life. A rich spiritual life is reflected in an inner peace, serenity, a quiet confidence and a more grateful and joyful way of living. This is not an issue of religion. It is a matter of letting God work in and through us. We focus on what is right. We see the big picture. We realize that life and death are connected and accept the impermanence of life.

With this perspective in mind, my goal is to be healed. That may not include being cured. Being healed is being at peace with where I am now.

The trauma in my mind and body stopped me from pursuing my creative, artistic spirit that I was my core for fear I would be poor, criticized and misunderstood all my life. I had to take the risk and be the person I was meant to be in spite of the risk and my fears.

Art Beckons

The sun beckons and promises a day of abandon
My oil paints call to me
The bills and "to do" lists can wait for another day.
Yet a strong force keeps me glued to my chair
Promising an approval that is always just beyond reach.
I sit in my chair watching
As the sun sets,
Gradually losing its luster.

God saved my life. He gave me a second chance for a reason. But when God bestows a second chance on you, you have to be the one that follows the treatments God leads you to. You have to love yourself enough and have the desire to live in order to take the steps you need to get your health back and return yourself to good health. You need to follow the treatment plan you are shown and follow it for the rest of your life.

God led me to alternative methods of healing. But I also feel he led me to the right surgeon to remove my breasts. That is what I needed to do to have peace of mind. I know now after doing my research that surgery didn't really get rid of my cancer and most likely caused the leftover cancer cells to travel in my body. But I believe that I can still reverse the process that started the cancer so these cells do not grow into another tumor. Getting the surgery done gave me the time to think about my next step and get to the point of trusting God totally to show me what I needed to do next to heal myself.

Soon after I was diagnosed, I had a feeling throughout my cancer journey that I would not die from the disease and that God was with me every step of the way. But this deep faith did not come overnight. I had reflected on, questioned and matured my faith for many years, partly with the help of a spiritual director.

Faith begins where knowledge leaves off. When my doctor became unavailable right around the time my six-month check-up was due, I panicked. But it forced me to do what I could to find ways to heal myself. Now I see it as a God-send. It got me out of the conventional medical system, which entails constant tests, check-ups, pressure to follow conventional treatments and taking toxic drugs, and forced me to rely on what I could do for myself to heal.

At that time, I didn't schedule an appointment with my doctor and now I had no choice but to go on my own as I had no more health insurance. I know many people will disagree with this choice and I am not here to argue with them. Everyone has to make the choice that is right for them. I have a right to share my decisions and process I went through, and hopefully they will help someone who is making similar choices.

If I am meant to die, I plan to do it on my terms, living with a good quality of life. It won't be spent in hospitals or doctor's offices, waiting to see the test result is to see if I can start living my life. I choose to live my life now no matter how long it is to be.

In the book *I See Your Dream Job*, a double "11" (which I am) is a master spiritual number.[7] It means you made a promise to God to come back to earth to fulfill the mission you decided on and have committed to fulfilling. You set it up so you could not turn back. You had to move forward and do what you promised. This is when you develop health issues, or get fired, or voluntarily leave from a long-term job. You must shed old beliefs, relationships and patterns that no longer work for you. You are required to step up to the next level of your great work. You realize you only have a few productive years left to fulfill your potential so it is now or never and you feel a sense of urgency.

I believe I was saved so I could write this book and maybe save other people's lives who were led to this book.

For me, I felt God's presence and guidance throughout my journey with cancer, the decisions I made were right for me but did not necessarily make sense to the world. I had a strong faith, but I had never really let myself rely totally on God. Until I was able to do this, I realized God could not work the miracles needed to heal me. It was my total brokenness that allowed God to penetrate the depths of my heart.

---

[7]   Sue Fredericks, *I See Your Dream Job: A career intuitive shows you how to discover what you were put on earth to do* (New York, NY: St Martin's Press, 2009), 41

At times I doubted God's promise to protect me because I didn't think it was fair that I survived when others didn't. But it was not up to me. God had a plan for me and I needed to be here. It really was none of my business what God had promised others. For some reason, I was chosen to survive. Perhaps to help others through their journey by writing this book. The good work God had begun in me was not finished.

Purpose

When I listened to my spirit I knew what to do: my choice of surgeon, my treatment decision, the scheduler for my MRI, the lovely nurses who held my hand during my biopsy, the therapist who helped me deal with the emotional aspect (a breast cancer survivor herself) and all the people who came forth to help me and my dog Spark as I went through recovery. It was frightening experiencing so many procedures and huge decisions I was not prepared for. But I always had the sense that I would not die and that each step was pre-determined, I would be fine.

Even though I believe that I am cancer-free, a little voice creeps up at times and tries to get me to doubt what I know to be true. I don't plan for five years out anymore. I don't know how many years I have left. So I plan ahead but I always keep God at the center now. I listen to the small voice inside me and to follow God's guidance, not my own. For example, a year after my surgery, I quit my job and went out on a limb totally on faith after praying for months about what path would be best for me and my health.

When I finished with surgery, I knew in my core God had healed me. I was a survivor, not a victim. But the world doesn't see things that way. You continue to be tested. I refuse to be in the system the rest of my life waiting for the word that I am ok or not when I know I am fine. I know I have to be the one to take charge of healing myself.

Healed by Nature

When I was about nine years old, we lived near a small creek. I used to go there almost daily and sit on a small wooden bridge and dangle my legs over the water and sometimes put my bare feet in the cold wetness.

The water gurgled over boulders and the noise soothed my soul. The trees surrounded me with their huge trunks and green leaves and I felt protected. The sunlight penetrated the spaces between the leaves, creating a mosaic of shadow and light.

Day after day, I sat on that bridge and watched the movement of the stream and the shifting light and listened to the birds sing. This was my sanctuary and it started my love affair with nature. Being in nature was the way I healed from many of my traumas and where I felt closer to God. The rich smell of soil filled my nostrils and lungs. I wanted to keep this sense of peace forever. As Hippocrates said, "Honor the healing power of nature."

I did not tell anyone about my secret place but many years later I started writing what I call "soul poems" and myths and this was my way of sharing the gifts and lessons I found along the way in life.

So when I got cancer, it brought me back to my need to find a place of peace. To find God in nature once again. The darkness that came uninvited brought me to an unknown, frightening place. The daily stresses of my life and work had taken over my senses and I barely came up for air except for writing an occasional poem and taking short walks in nature with my dog, Spark.

Once I got over the shock and outrage that this monster had invaded my body, my faith brought me back in balance. A new space was formed in my heart, one that was filled with the belief that my life would continue—it would just be different than before. I began to see the disease as a teacher that had come to remind me where I needed to find my peace. I needed to find the sanctuary I had created as a child and create a similar place within myself and to learn to manage stress better.

I had gone through many traumas in my life and also received excellent help from qualified health care professionals and therapists. So when I experienced the trauma of being diagnosed with cancer, I was able to eventually re-frame suffering without pretending it wasn't there.

One way I did that was signing up for an oil painting class. Painting was something I had wanted to do for a long time but kept putting off.

To my delight, painting helped me see objects as they really were and helped me break through any denial that still lingered. At my core, I am an artist, but was too afraid to express this part of me. I had been brought up to believe that art was frivolous and hard work was the only credible way to live one's life. Facing my mortality freed me up to explore the artist in me. Because I grew up with the message I must always be hard working and responsible, I shoved my artist-self deep down and forgot about her for years. If you shut out pain and suffering, you shut out everything. By going through the pain, feeling it, speaking aloud about it, I could find and experience joy. By expressing my truth through my art, I changed not only my own reality, but other's as well.

The Joy of Butterflies

Wrapped in a cocoon of worldly demands
She is totally focused.
Time slows as she gathers all her energy
For the task at hand
Life is Serious
It demands all she has.
A gentle breeze allows her to loosen her grip.
Making all her twists and turns seem effortless.
After years of toil, her
Cocoon of hypervigilance is broken
Joy, free as a butterfly
Bursts forth.

I would have rather not gone through this cancer journey, but by doing so I gained the strength to hang on. On the other side of strife and pain is true freedom and grace.

Trust Vs Worry

As I have grown and matured in my faith, I have become more heaven-centered than earth-centered. Heaven-centered to me means being God-centered and seeing God's higher purpose in my life. God has already given me the resources I need and waits on me to ask and implement. My priorities have shifted to become more service-oriented.

Earth-centered is human-centered and it is filled with worry and anxiety and self-ambition.

My Spiritual Journey

I said to my being,
Leave home, and live without hope
For hope must be for the right thing at the right time
Live without love, or you will love the wrong thing or person
At the wrong time
Live without faith, so it can be true
Let the hope, love and faith evolve in the time of waiting.

At the end of childhood, we are called into more responsibility. If we don't make this passage, and if we don't leave our childhood home—whether physically or emotionally—we won't mature. We are faced with the choice to leave home again and again throughout our lives, in many different ways, whether old certainties need to be released, or even abandoned entirely. I have constantly been faced with leaving old relationships, beliefs, jobs, memories and homes behind as I continue to grow and change.

For me, leaving home meant becoming more open to God. To mature spiritually, I had to strip myself bare and redefine what religion and spirituality meant to me: to no longer let patriarchal teachings passed on to me by people and institutions rule how I saw God.

Perhaps the only decision we don't have to face when leaving home is when to do it. It happens when a hidden desire stirs us into action. What used to be comfortable and secure now seems dangerous and confining.

Flying the Coop

I had to experience a "dark night of the soul" and lose my way before I could come home. To leave certainty to go to a place of uncertainty, we must be at a place of being brave enough to withstand family, financial and social pressure, and to be able to surrender to the process. If we can't withstand the uncertainty and pressures, we will turn to whatever addiction keeps us from hearing the silence and the truth. We have to be willing to wait and to trust whatever comes to light from out of the darkness.

When I made the decision to move to a nearby island, I had to force myself out of my comfortable cocoon where I had isolated myself almost to the point of being a hermit. Restlessness and the instinct for flight were my only guides. Looking back, I was in desperate need of a room of my own, or for my own voice. I was just going through the motions in life and not fully participating. I was slowly dying and my body was breaking down as a way to warn me.

I had to leap over a spiritual wall, not a physical one, in order to find the life that was meant for me. I had to find a spirituality that worked in the world. I had to let go of the need for my image of a male God who would take care of me rather than a being with no sexual identity who was a co-creator of my life. I had to learn to fly and test myself to see where my spiritual depths were. Just as Persephone descended to the underworld to lose her innocence and false sense of security in order to be reborn, I had to descend into my own dark place to learn the lessons I needed to learn. God became a force inside me rather than someone "out there" or found only in a church.

Church Parting

I have sought you in
Churches
Creeds
Rituals
Required statements of beliefs
I have tried to connect with you
In the eyes of the nice church ladies
Bible studies
And overzealous church greeters.
I have longed to feel your presence
By drinking your blood at communion
When I couldn't find you,

I thought I just wasn't trying hard enough.

Now I know I was looking in the wrong places.

Facing the Darkness

I had to learn to face the darkness and not be afraid of it on my spiritual journey. Christian liturgy focuses on the light and the message seems to be that if you are in the dark, you are not with God. As children, we are taught to fear the dark.

I was faced with the darkness when I got ill and experience it whenever anything scares me, which includes what it will be like to die, the absence of God and that the world is falling apart. Before, I denied my fear and tried to avoid the darkness or ran away from it. But now I turn towards the darkness and try to find the divine mystery within it. I pray to a God that is complex and hard to understand and I trust what guidance I am given. I am too religious for the spiritual but not religious enough for the religious crowd. I now see my questions and doubt as part of my spiritual journey and not as a lack of faith.

CHAPTER EIGHT

Finding my Voice
and Re-discovering God

"It took quite a long time to develop a voice and now that I have it, I am not going to be silent." – Madeleine Albright

> As a woman, I have been asleep.
> I have been unaware of the way women have been devalued, wounded and limited
> By culture, the church, and their families
> As a woman, I have been silenced
> Sometimes by husbands, other times, my father, male colleagues, or clergy
> As a woman, I am waking up
> A memory here, a thought there, an insight or recognition
> Of the powerful, sacred female inside that can no longer be ignored.

I was almost fifty-nine when I woke up as a woman, as a person of power. I had been programmed to be a sweet, soft-spoken woman who didn't talk back or speak up, no matter how bad the behavior presented to me. I swallowed enough defiant words to fill several rooms.

My health issues taught me that I needed to take my power back, to listen to and care for my own body rather than give power to doctors or anyone else for my healing. I was brought up to be "nice" and avoided conflict at all costs. My anger became focused on what it was to be a woman in this patriarchy and the lack of support I had gotten from my mother and from the church I had attended for so many years which did not value women as highly as men.

Rages Power

I ask God that this blessed rage
Not be contained any longer
But that I be given the strength
To burst the container that keeps it bound.
I ask for the grace
To gather the broken pieces and form
Not guards around its danger
But a path through its transforming power.

When we restrict our emotions, especially the aggressive ones like rage, cancer can grow inside us- it grows because we have chosen to not grow emotionally. I began to see that rather than turn my rage inward, I needed to turn my rage towards the processed food industry, the pharmaceutical industry, the health insurance system (which rewards illness by penalizing those who take preventive methods to care of themselves) and the pesticide industry instead.

It is difficult to grow up as a woman of substance in this culture, especially in the traditional church, where the popular images of women in the Bible have been portrayed as temptresses, prostitutes and the source of sin and suffering in the world. We are often seen as frivolous, intellectually deficient and as second-class citizens. The messages I picked up from my family and culture were:

- be silent
- put others first
- disindentify yourself with your body, senses and feelings
- turn inward to be safe

My wakeup call was called Cancer. It gave me the permission to start doing the things I was inhibited from doing before.

I could no longer watch bright and competent women, including myself, be overlooked or even rejected because they were strong, confident or creative. I had no choice but to grow up and become an adult to take responsibility for my ideas and start putting them out into the world.

> The life I have held faithful to beckons
> The luminal time full of awkward disconnections and turmoil
> Spurs me on to reach for what I have wished for on paper.
> A new sense of belonging drives me
> To unclench my rigid hold on the past and to find ease
> Oh to be free of this desert time!
> To finally be able to see and celebrate
> The life I have sacrificed everything for.

Becoming an Extraordinary Person/Patient

You aren't taught how to become an extraordinary person or patient in school. It took the hard knocks of life to refine me. It took me a lifetime of trauma, loss and disappointments to change my life and do whatever it took to make myself whole and healthy. In the past, I did work in teaching and life coaching to help others, but I was too wounded myself to give my all to my work. So I burned out on what I now know to be my calling. Teaching is a way to heal, inspire and motivate myself and others. I realize now that whoever I teach or help teaches and heals me more. But I needed to make a decision to teach on my own terms in my unique way. I needed to take the time to figure out what kind of teacher I wanted to be.

So I took a break from teaching and went back into sales. I sold advertising for over two years and built my confidence and skills while I worked on my emotional well-being through therapy. I made enough money to pay off most of my debt and even save a little. I met many wonderful people who were clients and several became good friends. I tried to make the best of a very demanding and stressful job and environment and I learned how sustain my spirit within the corporate setting.

It wasn't until I got cancer that I woke up. I realized I needed to get back to teaching in a new way. My sales job was making me ill. I needed to share my story as a way of healing myself and maybe helping others, while protecting my heart from those who tried to steal my strength and light.

In the past, when students or clients shared their pain, I withdrew because I was hurting. I pulled away when they needed me most because I hadn't yet learned how to protect myself or separate my pain from their pain. I needed to learn how to express my feelings without impairing my ability to make decisions so I could be a good example to my students. Going through a life and death situation clarified my gifts and talents and I knew I could no longer live without expressing them. I could allow myself to be more unguarded and real, as I now knew how to set boundaries and use whatever pain, conflict or situation that came up as a "teaching moment." Indeed I could draw strength from my students. They were the ones saving me, not the other way around.

Being an extraordinary cancer survivor has transformed me into being an extraordinary teacher. Both require that you do whatever it takes to open up the unconscious. I had to be willing to live an authentic life, an undivided life.

Parker Palmer explains one's journey to authenticity, or being "divided no more."[8] In the first stage, individuals make an inward decision to live authentically. The gap between their inner and outer lives becomes so painful that they resolve to find a center for their lives outside of institutions. They may leave the institution or stay, but they abandon the "logic" of the institution, or take a spiritual leave vs. a physical leave. Many people give up in the face of institutional resistance, but others seem to find a source of energy in the resistance and ask, "Why" and "How can things be changed?" They see the resistance as helping change happen and the resistance itself as pointing to a need for something new.

---

[8] Parker J. Palmer, *The Courage to Teach: Exploring the inner landscape of a teacher's life.* (1st ed.) (San Francisco, CA: Jossey-Bass., 1998), 173-189.

Because we are in the habit of seeing institutions like schools and churches as harboring opportunities we value, we find it hard it to leave. But sometimes these claims are at odds with our hearts (i.e. the inward imperative to speak up when a company does something unethical).

Stage Two, called "Communities of Congruence," happens when individuals who have reached stage one start finding each other and offer mutual support and opportunities to develop a shared vision. They provide a safe place to experiment with their language of the heart so they can communicate it to the public realm, which may be skeptical or hostile.

In Stage Three, "Going Public," these communities of congruence become strong. They learn to convert their private concerns into public issues, and they receive necessary criticism in the process, which helps them refine themselves.

In Stage Four, "System of Alternative Rewards," an alternative system of rewarding emerges that sustains the movements' vision. They use some of what the institution they left used but in a new way. Some of the rewards may be the benefit of living an undivided life, learning more about their own identity, and being in community with like-minded people. Having integrity is seen as more important than having money, raises, promotions and status, or the things organizations use to reward us. These people have come full circle – they are again co-creators (vs. victims) and they put pressures on the institution to change.

Divided No More

An Undivided Life Out in a field beyond Right and wrongdoing
I found communion with strangers Dare I say "I found love"
I practiced patience and kindness I lived in the tension
I used laughter and silence to fill the gap.
I was dissolved and shaken and I became more myself.
As I prepare to leave this field, my heart breaks I pick up the shattered pieces
And create a large well

Where I can hold more of my own and the world's suffering
I can now say my life means something real
Because of the kindness and love of others

Finding a Support System

I have never been good at asking for help and once I became open to getting help, I had a hard time finding it. I had always been the one giving the help, encouragement and strength to others and I had to learn to receive these things from others. Often people would say they wanted to help, but when I asked them, they would be busy or not show up. A few times I confronted these people and told them that I really needed their assistance so they needed to fulfill their promise to me. But the bottom line was, I had to find a different type of person - ones who did what they said they would.

I had some wonderful friends but none that had experienced cancer. It was important to me to have some like-minded cancer survivors that I could go to for questions and encouragement. I found that support about a year after my diagnosis. My therapist told me about a nonprofit group where you could attend a cancer survivor retreat for free if you were currently under a doctor's care.

I went not knowing what to expect and feeling a bit anxious. But my small group was the perfect group for me. I shared a poem at our first group that put me out there in a very vulnerable state and it seemed to open everyone up and our truths started to flow right from the start. It is as if we knew we did not have time to waste and needed to cram every moment full and ask for what we needed. We shared about our feelings of loneliness, fear and anger, as well as, our individual ways of dealing with the disease. We let down our defenses and shared from the heart. We cried, we laughed, we danced and we hugged.

We realized that each one of us was wounded and handled this in our own unique way that we no longer needed to be ashamed of it as there was nothing left to hide. For some of us, it was the first time we had experienced the reassuring peacefulness of such trust.

A miracle occurred. Something that could take months or even years happened within moments for us. We opened up and connected on a deep level. We didn't have to experience this journey alone anymore. I saw women who came in with an angry chip on their shoulder transform before my eyes in a few short days into loving, delightful people who I wanted to be close to. I learned from one woman in the group how to face death with grace and acceptance. The peace she had shown out of her eyes and most of the time she seemed as if in some ways she already had one foot in heaven. She was not afraid.

The feelings of peace and love I found at this retreat stayed with me for a long time. I am a better person for having learned, thanks to this wonderful group of breast cancer survivors, to confront my fears, express my inner feelings and to experience my relationships with more authenticity. It helps me stay away from feelings of depression and anxiety and keeps my desire to live strong.

I searched for a similar community close to where I live but I asked for even more. The community I attracted is a group of women who stand by me, reflect back to me how much I am and how much I am here to share. Who believe in me, who I can tell my truth too with transparency and raw honesty and with whom I feel safe. Who love and support me no matter what our differences. Women who wish the best for me. Who help me remember who I am and what I came here to do. Who challenge me when necessary but in a kind way. They are there for me when I need help, whether it be a ride, food, etc. They pray with me. I can read my soul poems to them.

Circles of Trust

Circles of trust include the following touchstones:

- Extend and receive welcome.
- Be present as fully as possible.
- What is offered in the circle is by invitation, not demand.
- Speak your truth in ways that respect other people's truth.

- No fixing, no saving, no advising, and no setting each other straight. That mean when people speak, there is no adding to, changing or clarifying what they say.
- Learn to respond to others with honest, open questions.
- Attend to your own inner teacher.
- Trust and learn from the silence.
- Observe deep confidentiality.

As my friend Janice was dying of cancer she encouraged me to find my "tribe," the people who would be there for me like her friends and family were there for her. So I put a posting on a well-known site where I lived seeking my community, my circle of trust.

Seeking

I am looking for my spiritual community, my "tribe," my circle of trust. I am a person of deep faith. I describe myself as a spiritual and also a religious person who has done extensive work to make peace with my Christian upbringing. I am looking for women who will stand by me, who believe in me, who I can tell my truth to with transparency and raw honesty and feel safe. Who love and support me no matter what our differences are. Who help me remember who I am and what I came here to do. Who challenge me when necessary but in a kind way and are willing to pray *with me*.

I got an immediate response from about ten people. When I had my recent surgery two of these women came to the hospital with me and waited while I got my surgery. One of them drove me home, gave me a reiki treatment and stayed with me most of the day to take care of me. This is what I have needed in my life and because I asked for it, it is happening for me.

Re-framing my Disease

Statistics say that one in four die from cancer. I choose to think of it that three people of out four live. Why not be one of the three who live?

I have finally have realized that I am not immortal. I am only human. Cancer can happen to anyone and it happened to me. But even though I am not sure what the future brings, I plan to make the time I have as healthy and joyful as I can make it. I am not one of those who can say it is over and I am moving on. I am taking it as the wakeup call I needed to totally change my life in every aspect and remain mindful that if I go back to old habits, the cancer could come back. I chose to save my life right up until the end.

I try and do an act of kindness every day. I now see the vast difference between being "nice" and being "kind."

Living out my Calling

I am a teacher, but I do not follow institutional practice. I teach on my own terms. Growing a pair of balls has allowed me to be a more exceptional teacher. You don't choose your calling, it chooses you. I have tried to quit teaching several times when I get burned out, but it keeps showing up in my life. Because I was wounded, I was not as good a teacher as I could have been. But when my mask of "being fine" cracked, I rediscovered my inner light, the part of me that was never fully extinguished.

We teach who we are. There are moments of light and joy when I truly see the light turn on in students' eyes. There are moments of absolute despair when I feel like I am not making sense and even doing students harm. The way I teach comes from my inwardness, for better or worse. So it takes courage to put myself out there over and over. I learn about myself, and hopefully, if I can teach with integrity, identity and an undivided self, I can pass this on to my students. I just have to keep at it as it is who I am.

The thing about finding one's voice and speaking out and even becoming successful, there are consequences. I need to get out of my comfort zone. I will become accountable to share what I know and I will be challenged. I will be visible, under scrutiny, open to criticism, and maybe even ostracism. There will be people who disagree with me or who won't like me.

I can't sit home, hiding and watching TV anymore. More people may want things from me, such as wisdom, strength and money. It will take some getting used to. I am so used to struggling; it will be a new feeling to actually reach my dreams.

CHAPTER NINE

Getting Real and Growing a Pair

I always figured that the way to God was "up" but now I know the way to God is "down." Down to the depths, the darkness, the places where we don't want to look or bring to light. The journey for me has been up, down and all around and it probably always will be. I glimpse my true self and live that way for a while. Then I lose my way again and go back into the darkness and yearn to find the light again.

The thing that makes it different is that now I know I can experience joy no matter where I am on the journey. I have the tools now to get out of the darkness quicker. I also stay true to myself for longer stretches of time. What has helped is sharing the details of the dark times, although it can be very painful.

Because I have such a strong desire to heal myself and be whole, and for others to know who I am, I keep on with this pattern. I continue to allow myself to be more vulnerable and speak more directly about myself. It gets easier to be transparent.

But what does it mean to be real? Margery Williams says it best in The Velveteen Rabbit:[9]

> "'Real isn't how you are made,' said the Skin Horse. 'It's a thing that happens to you. When a child loves you for a long,

---

[9]   Margery Williams, *The Velveteen Rabbit* (Kansas City, MS: Andrews & McNeel, 1991), p. 2

long time, not just to play with, but REALLY loves you, then you become Real.'

'Does it hurt?' asked the Rabbit.

'Sometimes,' said the Skin Horse, for he was always truthful. 'When you are Real you don't mind being hurt.'

'Does it happen all at once, like being wound up,' he asked, 'or bit by bit?'

'It doesn't happen all at once,' said the Skin Horse. 'You become. It takes a long time. That's why it doesn't happen often to people who break easily, or have sharp edges, or who have to be carefully kept. Generally, by the time you are Real, most of your hair has been loved off, and your eyes drop out and you get loose in the joints and very shabby. But these things don't matter at all, because once you are Real you can't be ugly, except to people who don't understand."

Radical Self Care

Getting real for me involves radical self-care, or being mindful of how I care for myself. Even after all the changing I did to my nutrition, exercise, supplements, I had to take it a step further in order to heal from cancer. I had to commit to facing my inner demons and find out what thought process I need to correct that has made me sick. This involved intensive body centered therapy that helped me replace negative beliefs with positive beliefs. But first, I had to bring the negative out in order to deal with it.

I had to deal with my family issues, forgive my dad, and learn how to love myself. It is not a task for the weak-hearted. It took everything I had, but I knew it had to happen in order to save my life.

I had to grow a pair. That included setting boundaries and facing the truth about myself and my life. I, like many people, was living a life of duplicity: I worked at a stressful sales job that did not nurture me, but was slowly killing me. When we live like this, we affect our health. Our souls suffer when they are constantly violated. We must look at what is going on in our lives and what is keeping us from being inauthentic.

I had to look at how refusing to forgive had been a catalyst for my illness. And then I had to go about the business of relaxing, becoming authentic and forgiving. I put together a team to help me do this: a therapist, an acupuncturist/Chinese doctor, naturopath, a massage therapist, a reiki master and a group of strong, supportive women. I had to ask my body what it needed in order to heal. For me, it was quitting my job and going back into teaching. It meant continuing to work on my book and finishing it and starting a self-care blog. It meant expressing my creativity by writing my soul poems, taking a painting class and creating new recipes. I needed to stop worrying about things I could not change and change my mind about how it responds to money worries and stress.

It also meant crying a lot of tears, feeling my feelings and speaking up when I experienced or witnessed an injustice. As I continue on this journey of self-care, I try to be gentle with myself. It took many years to create the negative beliefs and lifestyle habits. It will take a while to undo the years the locust ate.

I am the one who knows my body. It just took me a long time to start listening to it. I don't need a doctor to do that. A doctor should act as your partner, to educate you on what you don't know or understand.

What I have learned is it is not enough to eat nutritious food, exercise and take supplements. I need to also set boundaries, live in alignment with my true self and core values, do what I love and am passionate about and surround myself with a loving community. My tribe consists of people who are committed to self-care and healing the world.

I decided to write my own prescription rather than let a doctor tell me what works to make me healthy.

My Prescription for Self-Healing

Support

I am healing myself physically and emotionally with the help of trusted professionals (EMDR therapist, acupuncturist, naturopath, massage therapist, reiki master). I will stay away from doctors that disrespect alternative treatments/ practitioners. It shows a dysfunction in the healthcare system and a doctorial, condescending, hierarchical mindset.

Beliefs

I am in the process of eliminating negative beliefs and people and replacing them with positive beliefs and people. The EMDR and Somatic therapy were hugely instrumental in this process. It actually replaced the negative with the positive using body centered therapy, through my right brain.

Spiritual

I continue to be my authentic self in all aspects of life. The most difficult area for me to do this has been the workplace, as it is not set up to validate people's true selves. The culture values overwork and long hours, not work life balance so it must come from me to set boundaries. Workplaces need to stop shaming employees. They must encourage creativity, allow flexibility and foster positive interoffice relationships. They need to encourage people to do work they love. But the responsibility for this lies with the individual to find what they are passionate about and then do it without making excuses for it.

I need to practice radical forgiveness of myself and others. I need to meditate daily.

Work

Work is what we do with ourselves for most of the day, whether we are paid for it or not. It is up to me to spend my days doing work that inspires me and that I love. That is why I quit my sales job and started a pet sitting business. I also teach in non-traditional ways (i.e. facilitate my circle of trust). I also give reiki to people.

I am working through my resistance to living out my calling and express my creativity daily rather than spend my time worrying about money every day. I started a self-care blog. I will take writing classes and attend a writing group.

Money

I will repeat affirmations about money to end limiting beliefs. I will title 10% of my gross income.

I will stick to my budget.

I will remember that my source for prosperity is God, not people or circumstances. I will pay off the rest of my debt.

I will get clear on my financial goals and trust the process. I will make more money this year.

I will buy a new car this year.

Health

I will continue to eat organic, fresh foods and eat gluten, wheat, and dairy, sugar free and cut out bad carbs (grains) and drink less coffee (and the coffee I do drink must be certified organic). I will get regular reiki treatments. I will replace all cleaning and health and beauty products with natural products. I will dance often to loud music. I will write more soul poetry. I will do a series of cleanses every six months. I will lose at least twenty-five pounds to get under two-hundred pounds and stay there. I will walk 40 - 60 minutes a day at least five days a week. I will do yoga at least once a week. I will continue taking supplements and vitamins. I will eat primarily as a vegetarian. I will believe I can heal myself from all my health issues. I will become my own doctor and write my own prescriptions. I will learn to manage stress in a more positive way through doing yoga, meditation, walking, prayer and laughter, and by doing car screams to express my artistic, creative essence.

Car Screams

Sometimes,
When it all becomes too much
To bear
I climb into my car
Roll up the windows
And let out a piercing scream that would cause
Anyone within hearing distance to jump in alarm
That is my prayer for that day.

I will be an advocate for myself in the toxic healthcare system. It is a business and the bottom line is profit.

Growing a Pair

When I say I "grew a pair," I am not talking about the physical male body part. I am talking about telling the truth about yourself, your illness, and your life. I am not even making a distinction about masculine or feminine, as females can have the kind of balls I am describing. Having a pair of balls represents an attitude, a state of mind and a way of thinking and being in the world. "Growing a pair of ball" means facing the truth about oneself, your illness and your life. It requires you to go deeper so you can look at the real reasons you got sick. When we wake up and grow a pair, we return to our natural state of wholeness.

If I truly believe that God works in everyone, then I must speak my truth, whatever the cost. I can no longer avoid conflict. The good news is that I can write my way out of fear and illness with God as my partner. I can speak up when people attempt to put me in a box or silence me. I can tell my story. I can reclaim my body and I can move about the world freely and fearlessly, without apology. This journey has been a long and difficult one for me. But it is as if I am being resurrected into a new person.

Resurrection

I descend to the underworld as I rename myself as a woman
At each of the seven gates
I must strip myself of former trappings.
Until I stand naked, unafraid of the evil that surrounds me.
I look for shortcuts until I realize there are none
I must give up the fight to make it all go away
I look in the mirror and see a blossoming image
Of what I will be when I have been resurrected.

Getting cancer was what resurrected me by re-directing my life. It was the moment when I made the decision to no longer live the old way and seek the truth, no matter what the consequences. I have learned to face the disease with peace of mind rather than fear. I do not deny the illness, or the possibility of death, but I also refuse to dwell on it. Cancer is not a life sentence, it is just a word. It is sometimes a daily struggle to choose peace over fear.

When only the disease is treated, then a new illness may appear. If the whole person is addressed and treated, true healing comes. The person can learn to live comfortably and joyfully in spite of life's inevitable stresses. It is the effort of working towards the healing process that brings the rewards.

A big part of my change came when I started cutting people out of my life who did not value me or honor their commitments to me. I also began eliminating the negative and toxic people and environments in my life. People who focused on the negative only served to bring me down.

I decided I would be the kind of cancer survivor who would be confident that I would beat back the disease and be able to resume a normal life. I had to learn to overcome pressures and conflicts that could lead to a conscious or unconscious death wish. I had to develop a will to live. That meant living with a peace of mind and calmness rather than depression, fear and unresolved conflict. I believe that the state of my mind creates the state of my body.

I use humor to jolt myself out of my mindlessness and to promote new perspectives so I don't go back to bad habits. I meditate almost daily, eat right, do yoga, pray and read positive spiritual readings daily, write daily morning pages, exercise daily and get a good night's sleep every night. I am convinced that all these things are keeping my cancer from ever coming back. This is like practicing medicine without a license.

I have committed to living out my core values, whether at work or in my life. Most of us live a life of duplicity, especially in the workplace where conformity and silence are the unspoken code of conduct. This is bound to affect our health, as day after day, we say the opposite of what you feel. Our physical body, including our nervous system, can't be constantly violated and stay healthy.

Because I was not expressing my creative fire, cancer could not find an outlet so I write on a regular basis.

I am no longer the wounded child I was who saw God as an authoritative father figure. I have a mature, healthy faith that sustains me.

The biggest challenge for me has been to learn to love and adore myself as I was not given unconditional love growing up. I was taught that it was selfish to love myself. The extent we love ourselves determines whether we exercise, eat right, get enough sleep, smoke, take care of our homes and cars and even if we wear a seat belt.

I believe that I can cure the cancer with my mind but it takes time and it is not easy. It takes a lot of strength. We must connect with the divine spark within us.

Going through EMDR therapy right after my surgeries helped me deal with my emotions, especially my anxiety that the cancer may come back. It brought my unconscious awareness to my conscious awareness so I could deal with them. Sharing my fears and problems led to relief and healing within my body.

I also had acupuncture treatments twice a month right after my surgery, which helped my body and mind heal. The research I have done on cancer treatments has served to validate what I have intuitively known all along. But I wasn't willing to stick my neck out and speak the truth until now. That is what cancer did for me-I grew a set of balls! I know by voicing my opinions, I will open myself up to being criticized and attacked. I really don't care anymore. Maybe by speaking up, I will save someone's life. By learning how to heal myself, I can now help others heal themselves.

Because I was frightened and wanted the foreign substance growing in my body out, I chose to get my breasts removed. I still believe I did the right thing for me as the cancer had not metastasized. But the truth is (and I doubt any doctor or surgeon will admit this) the surgery itself causes the cancerous cells that are still there to be projected out into other areas of the body. Since surgery and anesthesia cause the immune system to be depressed for weeks and months afterwards, this gives the cancer a chance to grow somewhere else. When I figured all this out, I knew the only thing I could do is learn about what causes cancer so I could reverse it and defend myself against it coming back.

This is the key message I learned and want to share: If a post-operative cancer patient is in "remission," but has made no changes in diet or elimination of toxins to shut the cancer process down, there is a near certainty that the oxygen deficiency will continue and that new tumors will eventually be found, perhaps many years later when the person thinks they are "cured."

I am so frustrated with our health care system. It supports people staying sick rather than getting well because sick people make the system more money. The protocol is about managing disease instead of curing or preventing it. Why aren't we reversing disease or treating predispositions to disease?

Standard of care is what nearly all physicians are taught to follow. It means that the same treatment is given every time for the same disease, regardless of the individual's history or the context for the onset and presentation of their disease. Standard of care does nothing to determine why the disease developed or what predisposing circumstances led to the onset of the disease but instead focuses on managing the symptoms.

Health care is heavily influenced by pharmacies and managed care.

Speaking the Truth

Because I spent most of my life silent, it was a major deal for me to finally speak up and share my truth. The truth is the dogs I have owned are the beings I have felt closest to. My dog, Spark, was (and will always be) the love of my life. The love they give me shows me what it is like to experience God's love.

They love me no, matter what. If that makes me weird, I don't care. I love people too, I just love animals more.

The one person it took me a long time to forgive and love was my dad. Yet he was the one I was always the closest too so it was confusing for me. He was handsome and athletic and knew a lot of people. I overlooked his character defects for many years and refused to see how he wrought destruction on me and the rest of our family with his critical spirit. But when I allowed myself to feel anger and grief, I came home to myself. After years of therapy and conversations with friends, and a session with a medium where my Dad's spirit came through, I did forgive him. I like missing him and relishing the good qualities and memories he gave me. This process has played a major part in my healing and in becoming whole.

I may get really busy again and forget to take good care of myself and get sick again. People may attack me or dispute my assertions once I publish my book. There will be no turning back. Success may change who I am. I have observed many people let success change them, make them greedy or addicted to power.

On the flip side, I am ready for this. I have worked hard for many years to reach this state of being. I have done the emotional, spiritual, mental and physical work that I needed to do to become healthy and whole. I have a strong and mature faith. I am not alone. I have a wonderful support system. I have a good deal of resources and people willing to help me. I look back on my journey and realize how far I have come. I didn't know I was this strong. I was presented with an ordeal that many will not survive. I had to prove that I had what it took to come out on the other side.

The Hero's Journey

Several months after my first diagnosis, I had a vivid dream.

I was with someone who urged me to dive into the ocean. We swam deeply into the abyss and finally reached the bottom of the sea. At first, I felt safe there. I had to use the bathroom and was shown to a flight of stairs that led up to a toilet. When I was done in the bathroom, I came back to the main area of the cave and started to panic. How would I ever get back to the surface? I made myself wake up so I would not have a full blown panic attack.

When I told my EMDR therapist about the dream, she said it symbolized "The Hero's Journey." The journey includes crossing over some kind of threshold and facing our deepest emotions. By diving into the ocean, I was allowing myself to face my deepest fears. The cave represented the darkness I was afraid to face and the toilet represented elimination of old beliefs. At this point in my journey, I refused the call as I was too afraid to face all my emotions. But I would get another chance to do this later.

In order to become whole, I had to fall and take this hero's journey into the darkness to see that I was living an ungrounded life and was in denial. It frightened me. Cancer was the darkness that drove me underground. But this is where I finally could find my true calling.

The Hero's Journey is a rite of passage that helps us cross over into maturity. It is a threefold progression:

1. Separation
2. Initiation
3. Return

For me, separation was created by getting diagnosed with cancer for me. It is what allowed me to remove myself from distractions that were irreverent or destructive to my path.

We open the door, cross the threshold and return through the door from the other side, a different person. We leave the old life behind, receive a deep wisdom from whatever life experience we encounter, and then return home to implement whatever we have learned into our lives. For me, my journey with cancer taught me that life was not about avoiding darkness and death, but embracing them. The goal became deal with all past karma and ascend or "graduate" to my true home – Heaven, where I would live in my spirit form and not have to return to earth as a human being with a body.

A rite of passage is like passing through a tunnel, or in my case, into the ocean, through a dark passage. It is a terrifying experience and must be done alone and we fear there will be no life line to grab on to. But death must precede rebirth. The heroine's journey involves coming face to face with our greatest fear. We must do that of which we are most afraid. For me, this was facing the darkness and death. When I faced possible death, this included facing my fear of being criticized and ostracized. But on the other side was a life worth living. I was not really living before and this was no longer acceptable. I believe we are given as many lifetimes as necessary to conquer the challenge and finally live a fulfilling life. Ignorance, dependency and irresponsibility must all die so we can make way for balance, courage, independence and power. The newfound maturity becomes more important than old ways of being.

The ocean in my dream represented me going back to nature. I needed to relax and let myself be enveloped by the water and trust that I would be able to return to the surface. To let go of control and surrender to the process. To re-enter the world as my authentic self, a women with balls who was not afraid to speak up.

Here in the darkness, we must ask ourselves the right question, whether we get an answer or not. This question is at the heart of the heroine's journey. For me, it was "What is my purpose?" Had I agreed to get cancer twice in this lifetime in order to learn what it is to be a light and be a spiritual teacher, teaching others how to create balance and healing in their own lives? To get back to nature, to get back to God?

It is difficult to stand in your own truth when everyone around you is telling you that you just need to keep things as they are. I committed to having the courage to make God the center of my life, to live beyond security and safety.

Returning from the abyss can't be rushed. You must avoid all impulses, however unconscious, that may trigger a panic and cause you to return to your comfort zone. We can choose to refuse the call, but must eventually face it again and again and suffer until we choose to transform into a new state.

For me, I had to face the fear that I was not capable of handling my greatest fear death. I was helped by several people along the way who gave me crucial guidance. I needed to dispel my doubts and fears and give me the strength and courage to follow my quest. But in the end, I had to face whatever test, allies and enemies I was confronted with on my path alone. I had to learn who I could trust.

When I had my MRI after my first diagnosis, I discovered my fear of being enclosed in a tight space (out of control) without a way to escape. When I was told to go face down on the machine, my anxiety increased with each breath. I didn't want to stay in that dark, confining space (just like I didn't want to stay under the ocean with no escape plan in my dream). I felt like I was suffocating or was being buried alive. The smells and sounds of death overwhelmed me. I yelled out to the MRI technician that I wanted out. She argued with me that I was almost done and needed to stay put which just increased my anxiety. I yelled louder to her to "Get me out NOW!" At that time, I could not let go of control. I needed to get out in order to feel safe.

I had to experience a reoccurrence of cancer to finally learn to let go of the illusion of control. I had to face my deepest fear and realize that I was going to die, whether from cancer or something else, and that death was not something to be afraid of. Living a life of suffering where I was not truly living fully was something I needed to be afraid of.

My health issues have served to teach me that I needed to take my power back and to listen to and care for my body rather than give power to doctors.

After defeating the "enemy" and surviving some form of "death," we are reborn into a stronger person with increased knowledge or treasures of some kind. I came away with increased spiritual understanding and knowledge of how to go about healing myself. I came out on the other side with a sense of vindication that the path I had chosen was indeed the right one for me. I was even validated by my medical doctor who supported the path I chose. At this point, we must choose between going back to living an ordinary life of committing to a higher cause, leaving his old life and those in it behind. Having navigated the journey successfully, we return to everyday life as a different person with a new gift and often begin contributing to society.

CHAPTER TEN

Here We Go Again

Cancer is a nasty, tenacious disease. It wants to kill you. You have to decide whether you are willing to live and fight back. Unfortunately, two years after my diagnosis, I was forced to make this decision once again. I had to ask myself if I truly wanted to live until I am 100 years old, knowing life will bring me more pain and suffering, and knowing I may have to fight cancer again and again.

After two years of emotionally, physically, and spiritually rebuilding myself, it looked like the cancer was back. I found a lump along the scar on top of my skin where my right breast used to be.

Sometimes I wished I didn't know so much about the cancer process so I could live in denial and pretend that I am cancer-free. Because now I knew even that if I have a tumor surgically removed, it doesn't get rid of the cancer in the body. So I can never really say that I am cancer-free. I am a worrier by nature, so this fact causes me to worry even more, which is not good for my health.

On the other-hand, educating myself on the cancer process had empowered me. I have faced the truth about what I am dealing with. I can die from this and I must plan for my eventual death.

This was a sixth sense, an inner knowing. I had not yet gotten an official diagnosis. I was already prepared for the worst so if it turned out to not be malignant, I would at least know one way or the other. What this taught me is that my life will never be the same. I have a chronic disease I must manage diligently and mindfully the rest of my life. So whether

I did indeed have a malignant lump or not, I still have the cancer cells in my body. I have to always do what I can to keep them from forming together to create malignancies in my body. It becomes more important now to take my own health and healing into my own hands.

At first, I told a few select people who I knew would support me whatever I decided to do. In the meantime, I am on a strict vegetarian diet, with no sugar, no coffee, and I am doing a series of cleanses that span six weeks. I started with cleaning out the toxins from the colon, then Candida and parasites, then kidney and ending with my liver.

I had to face the truth. That no matter what I did to keep the cancer from returning, I have cancer and it must be managed the rest of my life. There were still lessons to be learned. I had started getting complacent, thinking I was cancer-free, so I could add back some sugar and processed foods and cheese to my diet. Wrong! Eating sugar grows cancer for one thing. I know this but I ignored it. Since I am a sugar addict eliminating it is a very difficult process.

One method I researched that may prove to be helpful is Vitamin C IV treatments. They build your immune system. When taken intravenously, vitamin C can reach much higher levels in the blood than when it is taken by mouth. Studies suggest that these higher levels of vitamin C may cause the death of cancer cells. They are not FDA approved and there is no proof they cure cancer, but I felt that they would help me. So I got one once a week for four months. I believe that they stopped the tumor from moving outside my body to inside my body.

One thing I am grateful for is that my big, fatty breasts were cut off so I could see and feel this lump. Before, I could not see or feel anything in my breast so I was unaware of what was growing inside my breast for years. Now I can see if there are any changes right away. When I was diagnosed the first time, it always seemed a bit unreal that I really had cancer as I couldn't see or feel it and I didn't feel sick. But this time, I could see and feel it so it was very real and I couldn't pretend it wasn't there.

The important thing I needed to remember is that I can't beat myself up. I believe many years of accumulated stress have taken their toll, not once but twice. I was now given a second chance to eliminate stress from my life.

Around this time, I read a quote by Sandra Bullock:

> "You can't go around just saying life is good. Because it is really a series of painful, disastrous moments that break your heart. They come unexpectedly, just when you think your life is easy and smooth. But in between those moments do come moments of joy when you can savor life until the next painful, disastrous time."

Is that enough for me? To have brief times to savor life? I have to say yes because I do love life and everything it brings to teach me, no matter how hard it is. No one ever promised me life would be carefree and problem-free. But somehow I felt that unless it was, I could not relax or feel joy. Now I know that whether this cancer kills me or not, I will die from something. I have to choose to live well; to live fully and not live being afraid every day of dying. The truth is, I will die, I just don't know when.

In the two years between reoccurrence, I learned to love myself. I lost my once-in-a-lifetime dog, Spark, but received my dear Brodie soon after to heal my heart. I found a job I liked and was good at and I boss who was wonderful. I couldn't believe I had finally found a great boss so late in life after enduring so many not so wonderful bosses. I loved my part-time, flexible schedule. My pet sitting business was growing and I could finally say I had a successful business- a long-time goal achieved. I have surrounded myself with strong, powerful, caring women who are there for me. The truth is, I am happy, and if it weren't for the cancer, my life would have been just about perfect. I refused to let cancer define me. It could take my body eventually, but it could never take my spirit.

For all the joy life has to offer, life also is full of loss and grief. Life is made up of shadow as well as light and to be fully human, we must embrace it all.

When my tumor reappeared, I talked with my best friend, Jenny, who was also a two-time breast cancer survivor and shared my fears and thoughts. She suggested I would feel better if I got a biopsy so I could find out one way or another if I have cancer. I already knew in my gut that I did, but maybe a diagnosis would help it become more real and I could move on. I did know, either way, I wouldn't go the conventional route and get chemo, radiation or take drugs. I would do whatever alternative treatments I could do that I could afford. I do not regret the path I took. I had lived two years feeling good before the tumor reappeared. I was not that person stuck in doctor's offices or hospital rooms or hooked up to a machine receiving chemotherapy.

I created a fundraiser on Facebook to help pay for my Vitamin C IV treatments as they are not covered by insurance. At the time, I worked part-time and was slowly growing my own business which was not yet sustaining me financially, so I needed to ask for help. I wasn't able to work full-time and go through this process. After only one week, I received $300.00 from friends and my landlord allowed me to live rent-free for as long as I needed to get treatments for 5-6 months. To see the wonderful spirit of people in my life who love me was so healing in itself.

This was another reminder that God is in control, not me. If I was meant to die from this, I would. If I am meant to live and learn more lessons, then I will be led to the right treatments for me. This was a chance to see if all that I have researched and believed heals, will really help me or not.

It is so hard to buck the system. In fact, insurance companies want to force you to do things the conventional way or they will refuse care. I feel so alone sometimes.

Did I regret all that I had done the last two years to fight this disease, just to have it come back? No, I had come so far and learned so much. I was not the same person. I was stronger. I knew I had what it took to buck the system and heal myself my way (God's way). By writing this book, I had learned that cutting out the tumor does not get rid of the cancer. It is a process that needs to be reversed or it will come back. I did my best to make sure that didn't happen, but obviously, I had more to do.

I felt where I had the most work to do emotionally. To rid myself of toxic people and situations in my life once and for all and to feel my feelings, then let them go rather than holding onto them. I had to stop being so fucking "nice" and stop putting everyone else before myself. I read somewhere that it is the "nice" people who tend to get cancer, so I am done being nice. I would rather be kind. As a result of this insight, I created a kindness challenge for myself. I performed an act of kindness act every day then recorded it on Facebook. It kept my mind off my health issues and on something positive and proactive.

It just pissed me off as my life was so good just before this happened. In spite of this set-back, I still felt my life was good, but added to that was a lot of anger. I didn't even feel like crying anymore. I just felt like throwing crap across the room and yelling at the fucking cancer to get the hell out of my body.

Around this time, I talked to my friend Janice and she said something that really resonated with me. She said the first time she got cancer it was on her, but the second time, it was due to several generations of women in her family bringing on the cancer to bring her down to their level because they saw her changing and growing.

I also felt some unresolved guilt and grief over my dog Spark's death. I am sure some of that had manifested into cancer. I did an exercise from a book on radical self-forgiveness that helped me release the feelings of guilt and sadness I was holding onto from Spark's passing. I also looked at the possibility that I manifested getting sick so people would show they cared about me. Since I have struggled with wondering whether people in my life truly care about me, this was a strong possibility.

I think where I went wrong is that I needed to be more serious about replacing the conventional treatments with serious alternative treatments. You can't just do the surgery and be done with it, even though I had done a ton of good things for myself. That was one reason I started doing the Vitamin C IV treatments and cleanses.

I knew if God saved my life a second time, it was for a reason. I would do whatever I was guided to do.

I continued to have the sense that God puts just the right people and just the right resources in my path at just the right time. I was referred to a new acupuncturist in town by my naturopath. I had been looking for one to replace the acupuncturist I saw for over eight years in Seattle. I got tired of the two-hour drive and had stopped seeing her.

I liked this new acupuncturist right away. She has such a beautiful, positive healing energy and she knew right what to do to help me that first night after we had talked for about fifteen minutes and I had let her examine my lump. She opened up my mind to get the biopsy just to be sure as it could be something else. As she reminded me, whatever the diagnosis is, it is my decision what I will do. I was already doing everything I can to help reverse the cancer, so the diagnosis would just give me some closure.

Dealing with Conventional Medicine Again

What is so interesting (and no accident) is that I went back to the same doctor who did my mastectomy to get her opinion on what I needed to do. I thought I would never see her again but we had unfinished business. I needed to share my disappointment about the way her office ignored me and never responded to my three attempts to make a follow-up appointment with her. Even though I am glad of the way things turned out, I still should not have been treated that way. She was extremely apologetic and we made our peace.

I was afraid I would be pressured to get a bunch of unnecessary tests—another mammogram, another MRI—and it would make me doubt myself. The insurance system is set up to require you to get certain tests done in order to get procedures done. But I ended up deciding just to get the tumor removed surgically and find out after the surgery if it was malignant.

I decided that if I found out the cancer had spread throughout my body, I would deal with that the best I could. This whole ordeal brought me face to face with death and what that means to me. My journey had become about not fearing death so I could live fully in the time I did have left. To live with a lightness and joy. I realized that I had not been doing that. I had been living by trying to outrun death. Doing everything I could think of to avoid facing it. But it is useless. Death will find me just as it does with everyone.

Here We Go Again

The surgery confirmed what I already knew: the cancer was back. For a moment, I wanted to take her suggestion and get radiation. But then I reminded myself about my commitment to stay the course and do things on my own terms. It brought the subject of death back to the forefront of my life. I would continue to try to live well in order to die well and continue to work on not being afraid of death.

I realized that I had been living in a way that is a reaction to cancer, from making sure it doesn't return. Now I had to live my life fully without letting cancer define me, but listen to what it had to tell me. I couldn't control what happened. I could do my best to live a healthy life. But after all my diligence, the cancer could keep coming back and I may die from it.

I needed to choose to live fully each day just because. Just because that is how I want to live. Rather than living each day in fear which is not really living. It is like walking around half-dead, never really enjoying life.

The thing is I like being a person on this earth. I have grown to like, and even, love, the person that I am and I don't want to end my existence on earth as the person I am now. I would get overwhelmed and wonder if I was doing all I could to heal myself and I felt alone in this process. I wondered if all I was doing was all for nothing. If it was my time to die, then none of this would matter anyway.

I guess I am just stubborn. I don't give up. I keep moving. I would keep fighting to save my life until I just can't anymore.

I had to believe the path that I had chosen was making a difference. That my instincts were correct and I could defeat this disease. If I stopped believing, then I might as well be dead. I just wanted more days when I could relax more and have fun and forget for that day that I had cancer. Then maybe, without realizing it, I would find myself on the other side of this, lighter than air, living the life I had always wanted.

CHAPTER ELEVEN

Fuck the Cancer!
(And Standard-of-Care)

Let me start by saying I was blessed to find an exceptional doctor who was a partner on my journey, not a dictator. She supported my decision to not go through radiation or chemotherapy. I did use Western medicine by getting surgery both times I had tumors. She changed after she got breast cancer herself (after my first diagnosis) and no longer pushed for her patients to get chemo or radiation although she got both because of the type of cancer she had. She was even willing to work in conjunction with my naturopath to do whatever she could to get me healthy.

But I felt stuck and angry at the universe and the Western drug regimen and treatments that may stop the growth of the tumor but can often make the cancer come back even worse. I was pissed that the medical establishment had nothing better to offer. I had to find something else. So I left Western medicine behind and sought alternative therapies. I resolved to heal myself.

I tried supplements, practiced restrictive diet plans, went to an acupuncturist and Chinese doctor who gave me tinctures to use. It wasn't until a friend offered to do reiki on me that I finally found something that seemed to miraculously work. Reiki is a form of therapy that uses simple hands-on, or no-touch, and visualization techniques, with the goal of improving the flow of energy. Reiki (pronounced *ray-key*) means "universal life energy" in Japanese, and Reiki practitioners are trained to detect and alleviate problems of energy flow on the physical, emotional, and spiritual level.

I also had to further refine my diet and resolve my digestive issues. I started back with the basics and wrote down everything I ate and surrounded myself with in my environment and sent it to my naturopath so I could adjust things as my blood tests still showed my body was inflammatory.

But getting mad at cancer and the medical establishment wasn't helping me to heal. Being angry is what forced me to learn to be my advocate and take responsibility for finding my path to healing. I was willing to go to great lengths and spend whatever money was needed to figure out what was right for me, and to find a treatment plan tailored to my needs and composition.

Maybe someday there will not be "alternative therapies," but an array of options which one's doctor guides you to find the right one for you. In the end, you become your own therapist, doctor, counselor and cheerleader. You must believe that there is something better out there for yourself so you never stop looking. For now, I have found it. But if I have to start looking again, I am up for the task.

Cancer Sucks!

Cancer is killing way too many. Why? Why is there not a cure with all the money being given towards research? The answer is that there is a systemic problem in our country that is a breeding ground for growing cancer. The pharmaceutical and insurance companies run the show. It is all about greed and covering one's ass. No one wants to spend the research money on exploring alternative treatments that work. So only conventional treatments are paid for by insurance, and these treatments cause more problems than they solve. If a treatment is not FDA approved, it will not be paid for. Things must change. All the money going to drug companies needs to be diverted to researching different cures.

Facing the Facts

Let's face it. One of the largest money producers for the traditional medicine establishment is cancer. Many doctors say they don't know the cause of cancer but there has to be a cause for every effect. It is a universal law. How can there be a cure when a cause has yet to be determined?

Conventional medical treatment of cancer is focused on the disease. The symptom of the cancer- the tumor- is attacked by surgery, radiation, chemotherapy and drugs or all of the above. Why is the person who has the cancer not addressed? Tests, often unnecessary, are given by techs that only care about the procedure, not the person. Many doctors and hospitals over test and over treat because they are paid for how much care they deliver and not how well their patient is cared for. They are reimbursed by each test and treatment they administer. Pharmaceutical companies want oncologists to prescribe more chemotherapy so they are paid more. Who is looking out for the best option for the patient? Why is there not more research that recognizes a tumor as an indication of an underlying imbalance? Getting rid of a tumor is not enough; the underlying imbalance must be addressed and reversed.

We are entitled to know the truth. We only hear about conventional treatments for cancer. Why don't we hear about unconventional treatments that actually prevent or reverse cancer?

The truth is that chemotherapy is poison. It may kill cancer cells but it also damages healthy cells. It also triggers the cells to secrete a protein that sustains tumor growth and resistance to future treatment. So it is the leading cause for secondary cancers as it causes cancer growth and affects long- term immunity. The risk for a second cancer may develop slowly over five to ten years. But diagnosis is inevitable. It not only destroys healthy cells, but our organs. It also compromises the immune system so we are more susceptible to infections and complications.

What seems to be kept quiet is that cancer cells can't survive in an oxygenated environment. Francis shared how Dr Otto Warburg discovered back in 1931 that when any cell is denied sixty percent of its oxygen, cancer occurs.[10] There are other causes but lack of oxygen seems to be the number one reason.

Oxygen is reduced in the cells by a buildup of cellular toxicity, poor blood flow (red blood cells clump together which slows down the bloodstream

---

[10] Raymond M. Francis, MSC, *Never Fear Cancer Again: How to prevent and reverse cancer* (Deerfield, FL, Health Communications, 2011), 63-65.

and restricts flow into capillaries) and an acidic environment in the body.

Standard of Care versus Integrated Care

There is no one cause for all breast cancers but standard-of-care protocol has doctors treat everyone the same. If they don't offer the standard of care options, they can be sued for malpractice. I believe also, that doctors and hospitals make more money the more treatments they provide, whether they are needed or not.

One question that came up for me is if there is no known cure for cancer, why are there treatments? The word "remission" means that it will come back, in spite of any treatments. Since there is no cure for cancer, you can't be totally cancer-free.

If we aren't aware of all the potential causes of cancer (from the toxins in the environment and the foods we eat, to the way we respond to stress, to genetics and many other causes) we tend to blame ourselves. In order to become an exceptional patient, I needed to stop blaming myself or others. I needed to re-frame my experience from self-blame to self-compassion and learn how to love and care for myself. For me, healing breast cancer is not about treating the illness, it is about creating wellness.

I am glad I had my surgeries as I feel that is what got out most of the cancer and saved my life, but I am not sure I needed an MRI, an expensive and nerve-wracking test to see if cancer is anywhere else besides the breast. Because of my trauma experienced during my MRI, I knew the medical system was a sham and that I needed to stand up for myself and say, "No. I told my doctor she would have to do the surgery without the results from an MRI."

What I had to confront was whether the benefits of conventional treatment for early stage breast cancer outweighed the risks which are premature death and reduced quality of life. I decided I would do everything possible to make my life better and make my immune system stronger by doing everything I could that did not cause me harm.

Cancer is a Process, Not a Thing

What I learned is that unless the cancer process is turned off, you still have cancer and it will only be a matter of time before it comes back. Because most cancer is slow-growing, this may take years. So many people have the false belief that they are "cured" but the truth is that cancer has moved to another part of the body and unless we start to do things differently in a major way, the cancer will multiply and grow. The survival rate for most forms of cancer was the same in 1995 as it was in 1950. Conventional methods can make things worse. In fact, doing nothing seems to be the best thing you can do to live longer and better *if* you are doing the right things to keep your cells and body health in its natural balance. By doing nothing, you are not creating further damage to your already sick cells.

The people doctors call "spontaneous remissions" are actually those who drastically changed their diet or went through detoxification or supplement programs. These substantially alter one's cell chemistry and shut down the switches and drivers that promote cancer. Through changing your diet, mental, spiritual pathways, you restore natural cell health.

Instead of using conventional cancer treatments that try to kill the cancer, we can choose to turn the cancer off by addressing the causes, giving the body what it needs in order to make itself well.

What made sense to me is reading Raymond Francis's book *Never Fear Cancer*, where he talks about how there is only one disease which is malfunctioning cells.[11] There is just one treatment: making the cells healthy again. All the different diseases are just the ways different people manifest the disease in different tissues and in different ways. The one thing that is common to all cancer cells is a deficiency of oxygen metabolism in the cell. This can be caused by things like processed oils, acidic PH levels, etc. So we must find the ways that will produce the oxygen needed to destroy the cancer cells.

---

[11] Raymond M. Francis, MSC, *Never Fear Cancer Again: How to prevent and reverse cancer* (Deerfield, FL, Health Communications, 2011), 63-65.

Radiation and chemotherapy don't work to get rid of the cancer. It will most likely come back because the process of cancer is still operating. The only way to win against the cancer is to turn the process off. We must address the causes at the cellular level and figure out how to restore the normal biological balance in our cells.

Cancer is not what causes us to be sick, it is toxicity and deficiency—in other words, it is an imbalance. If we lead a stressful lifestyle, stress chemicals deplete the body of critical nutrients, causing deficiency. An excess of stress chemicals has a toxic effect on the body. As far as being deficient, even if one raw material (nutrient) is chronically lacking, our body will not be able to make enough of the right chemicals. A chronic deficiency of even one nutrient will make us sick. A prime cause of all cancers is a deficiency of oxygen metabolism in the cells. Oxygen metabolism is the combining of oxygen with a fuel in a cell to create energy and heat. Normal cells have sufficient oxygen. Cancer cells are fueled by sugar fermentation. Chemotherapy and radiation reduce the amount of oxygen in the cells which is the opposite of what needs to happen.

When cells malfunction, thousands of symptoms can be produced. Which symptoms are produced depends on one's particular combination of deficiencies and toxicities and your unique genetic makeup. What we call cancer is merely a certain class of these symptoms—cells in different parts of the body, such as the breast, keep growing and don't stop. Different diseases look different from each other because they are merely symptoms produced by cells in different tissues that malfunction for different reasons in different ways. But it is all cellular malfunction.

There is only one treatment: restoring cells to normal function, which eliminates all symptoms. So we must simply change from the conditions that favor the cancer process to those that favor health. Once the deficiencies and toxicities are removed and the cells are restored to normal function, diseases can't persist. Not even cancer.

What I have learned in my research is the following:

Everyone has cancer cells in their body. Not everyone's cells will multiply enough (in the billions) to be detectable as cancer cells. So I am not sure we can ever say we are "cancer-free." We can just say that the cancer process is being managed. Many people's immune systems are strong enough to destroy the cancer cells and stop them from becoming tumors. Cancer is a sign of multiple nutritional deficiencies – what we put in our mouth, environment and lifestyle is crucial.

Who is in Charge?

Right now, the pharmaceutical and insurance companies are in charge. They make a lot of money off sick people. Alternative treatments take away the money and are not recognized by the FDA. But medications never get to the root of a problem; they just mask the true cause of the problem. True cures are found in nature, God's pharmacy.

CHAPTER TWELVE

Impermanence

Facing death was my greatest challenge as I dealt with a reoccurrence of my cancer at the same time as my best friend, Janice, was dying of cancer. Janice was an example to me of what it was to live well and die well. She taught me that dying is a natural progression of life. We just aren't part of a body anymore but our spirit or soul continues to live on.

I knew intuitively that if I were to be fully present for her in her dying, I had to face my own fears of dying in order to talk openly to her about how she was feeling about death. Whether it is a fear of increasing pain, suffering indignity, dependence, a fear of having unfinished business, that the life we have led has been meaningless, fear of separation from those we love, of losing control, losing respect or the fear of fear itself, we are all afraid of some aspect of death.

Watching her journey to death, I was confronted with my own death. I didn't know when it would happen, just that it would at some point, so I might as well face the truth and prepare for it. Around this time, I wrote one of my soul poems to express how I was feeling.

Letting Go as I Approach Sixty

I am not ready to die.
There's still so much I am here to do on this earth.
But I am learning to trust that death
Has as much to teach me as life does.
As I move toward detachment,
I experience a new freedom.

A sweeter grace as I learn to let go of all possible outcomes.
I am not ready to die.
But as I near sixty,
I turn my face toward the ocean
I get lost in the waves and tides as they replace time.
I learn to go with the changes as I look over blue water. I am
grateful for it all.
God's mercy
God's demands God's light
And for God's darkness.

Preparing for Death

Nothing is permanent. Impermanence is the only thing we can hold
onto besides faith. Even when I write or do reiki on myself, it can be
a way to try and control things, to avoid death. If I can do these and
other rituals in solitude, mindfully and practice acceptance of death,
there is a real hope of healing not only my body but my whole being. I
can accept impermanence and still relish life.

The key is to find a balance, a middle way and to simplify life more
and more—for example, to work and not get entangled in the job or
the politics. But as we slow down, we are forced to notice how control
is an illusion, and that we can't rely on our bodies that we have tried so
hard to keep alive and that our mind betrays us. I think to prepare for
death we must make peace with our lives and those in it. If we believe
in karma, then to generate a virtuous state of mind at the time of our
death can bring about a happy rebirth.

Meditation is one way of experiencing death while alive. Each loss,
pain, difficulty, obstacle and time of suffering can be seen as a teacher
about the truth of impermanence. Before I learned this, I saw each
loss as something I had to painfully endure rather than seeing it as the
blessing that it was.

I believe that miracles can happen and that we can be healed if we are
willing to go into solitude and follow a spiritual practice where we can

truly face ourselves and the face of death. When we can accept the connection between life and death, healing can occur.

Cancer can be a reminder that we have been neglecting deep aspects of our being, such as our spiritual needs. For me, it was the need for community. I didn't have a family that loves me the way I needed to be loved so I needed to create my own community –women who are willing and able to care for me.

I got off track when I started believing that I had to take possession everything I could; I got greedy with material things and food (when my body took on more than its share- overeating, purging self with unhealthy amounts of unhealthy foods.) I also didn't follow my heart and do what it wanted me to do. If you are not doing what you love, you die a little each day. Because I put others needs before my own for so long and didn't nurture my artist self, I did die a little bit every day.

Letting Go

As I continued on my journey, I saw how ridiculous it was to keep trying to hold myself up with just my own strength. The strain had taken a toll. I had always been supported by the love of God inside of me but I had been so busy trying to strive for control, that I didn't notice it. I could have at any time surrendered and relaxed into the loving arms of God but it took facing death to finally get there. Now I feel God most whenever I am in nature. In nature, I don't feel separate from my body.

Now I see silence as death. Silence doesn't protect me, it damages you. You must speak the truth whether you can change things or not. I have to choose every day to surrender all. To put aside my goals, desires and will for God's will. To embody the sacred. To love myself and do well for myself. To trust the light inside.

The Writer within Me

I have written off and on all my life. My mom used to tell me growing up that I was a good writer but the underlying message was, don't take the gift seriously. You must be a responsible person with a regular nine-to-five job.

Writing was my way to authenticity, of knowing my relationship with the world. It was my way of getting out my truths. My desire to write and get my truths out would re-surface again after a while, showing me I had to risk people's disapproval to follow my destiny. Writing helped me understand myself and heal myself from my dysfunctions. It took me getting cancer to finally take writing seriously enough to write and publish this book. I wrote it to save my own life. If it helps save others, then that is icing on the cake.

I write because I must. I do it because it helps me remember who I really am and love myself unconditionally. It keeps me away from death's door but also lets me make peace with death and know that when it does come, I will have fulfilled my destiny and can leave this earth complete.

So even if I don't have many years left on this earth, I plan to spend what time I do have doing what I love to do and living fully. I live as healthy as I am able. I try to be kind to myself and to others. Every time I quit a job and say I am going to "fly" and trust that God will provide for me, I only last so long before I get too anxious and go get some kind of job. At least I have graduated to working only part-time and work at a job that I enjoy for a good boss. But even this takes away from my authenticity. Lately, I have been listening to my intuition nudge me and tell me I need to let even this job go and follow my dreams to the fullest.

If I truly wonder if I only had a few years left to live, what would I truly want my life to look like? I would be running a successful pet sitting business because I love animals, be writing and publishing more books and doing reiki on myself, animals and people. I would tell my story to groups. I would live a simple life. I would be debt-free. I would be surrounded by people who are doing similar things in life. When I feel that tension and start worrying about money again, I will trust God to provide because He always has. I will work through the tension and stay the course. Even if I have decades left to live, I want to spend those years doing what I came here to do. There will be no more detours, side trips, excuses, distractions.

By facing the fact that I am going to die at some point, I have learned that often I will not get my way. Life is crazy, beautiful, unpredictable and sometimes horrible. And yet, it is also sometimes glorious and sweet. I can continue to live with unresolved problems and still feel joy. Everything passes away, especially the people and animals I love that I couldn't live without. I am still here for a reason so I'd better step up and make the most of what time I do have left. There is no more time to put off doing what I was put on earth to do. This is the time.

CHAPTER THIRTEEN

Living Out my Purpose, My Soul's Plan

Winged Protection

I go to bed each night
Desiring a calm soul,
Consoled and renewed
Enveloped in a safe haven under a canopy
Of purple-blue and pink wings
A gold beams shines through a crevice
Igniting my heart with warmth and love.
I sleep soundly, knowing that
I have brought light and renewal
To myself and others that day.
The beauty of my soul shines through what I do
Releasing wellsprings of nourishment and excitement
Never exhaustion or bland excuses
Each day I awake, finding
Hope in my heart, anticipating new dreams
Possibilities and promises.
I will never again settle for less.

Cancer pitted me against my greatest fears: losing control and/or death. Surrendering to my "calling" meant giving up control of what I wanted my life to look like. But my life was not working the way I wanted it to anyway.

Before I was confronted with my immortality, I was content to live with a chronic anxiety. I procrastinated for years rather than face the painful self-awareness and move through the resistance I had. I feared what the calling may ask of me, its consequences and responsibilities. After all, nice girls don't speak their minds and grow a pair of balls. I was frightened that I would be put in the spotlight, ridiculed and even hated for my views.

I also felt called to finally heal my relationship with my mom. The fear of losing her love made me give up on myself for years in order to gain her approval. Rather than live authentically, I was not living my life, but hers. It was a defense against death.

Sue Fredericks, in her numerology book *I See Your Dream Job,* says a major event happens when we are around age fifty-eight.[12] Around this age, I started feeling intense discomfort and tension, and I could not shake the knowledge that I was not using my gifts and was dying away in my present life and work. But I could not break away from my comfortable life and steady income. Health problems and the politics at work just added to the turmoil. I knew I was destined to be a writer and teacher but how would I pay the bills?

Then at fifty-eight, I got the cancer diagnosis, and I could no longer put off what I was put on this earth for, no matter how scary leaving my comfort zone was.

I planned to leave my job a year after my surgery. I started preparing for my new life. I paid extra on all my credit cards and paid my debt way down. I saved as much money as I could. I started networking with people I trusted to let them know I was leaving my job. I got my business license and liability insurance for a pet sitting job as I love and adore animals. I also edited all my life coaching and class materials so I could start teaching and coaching again, but in a new way. I took an oil painting class and wrote poetry. I started writing this book during every spare moment I could find. I started telling people about the book to

---

[12] Sue Fredericks, *I See Your Dream Job: A career intuitive shows you how to discover what you were put on earth to do* (New York, NY: St Martin's Press, 2009), 41.

see if they were receptive to it. Everyone I talked to said it was a great idea and they could hardly wait to read it.

Pieces of a Life

I take jagged pieces
Patches of darkness
And shape them into light.
I gather scattered wreckage
My hopes, fractured and whole, the struggles of birthing
And the places of greeting
And create a life
I lay these pieces at the threshold,
God and I ask you to bless them,
Tend them Mend them
Transform them, then use them
So they can make me whole
And I can be sent forth with a courage
And a faith that sustains.

A New Home

I moved to a new house just a few months after my surgeries. A friend had found this place for me and talked to the owner who was a friend of his and asked if I could see it. I was so out of it that I told him I could not even think about moving at that point. So I had to let it go.

A few months later, when I was feeling better, I ran into the landlord and she said the house was still available. I said I was interested, but was still too weak to pack and physically make the move. She said her family owned a U-Haul truck and if I could get some help getting packed, they would move me for just the cost of gas. I asked several friends over to help me pack and we did it over several days, and then my new landlord and her family moved me. It was the easiest move I have ever done.

I knew this house would be my dream place to live where I could write this book. It has so much character. It is one block from the beach and every window has a view of the water and is located where many artists

123

and writers live. I found a writer's group that meets weekly in a coffee shop which helped me stay focused on writing. My home is a healing place and I feel that I can be the artist I am at heart here.

Soul Shaking

Months after I left home,
It felt like something in my soul shook loose.
I couldn't describe what that looked like to her, so the next time we met,
I brought poems and drawings
The ones that told the truth about my life.
This, I told her, is what
My soul looks like shaking loose.
She told me that they needed a safe place to stay, so I gave then a special corner near my
Paints and oil pastels
And a beautiful notebook of their own.
These are the things of an artist!
I delight when I enter this space and realize that this is who I am.
You, who have helped reveal this name to me you, who breathe life into it daily,
This is the shape of a soul coming home now I know I will always have this space in different places
With different people Oh, blessed home.

Home (Soul Shaking Part 2)

Even before the time I moved in,
I knew this would be the home most mine
That this would be the space that would make me feel most at ease in my own skin.
Yet it has been the longest in taking shape,
The longest to feel like it is truly mine.
Almost a year after the move,
I told her that it felt like something in my soul was shaking loose again.

The poems and collages I brought to her
Were so much less precise now
With rough edges and torn shapes
Leaving room for the truth of my life to shine through the cracks
It seems as if my artist self has found a place to call her own
This space has helped reveal who I truly am-
And shapes the silhouette of a soul shaking loose and coming home.

I also had to learn to ask for help. I could no longer do it alone. I had to surrender to the fact that I am an artist at heart and I had no idea how I could pay the bills and create. Most artists have to work day jobs to support their lives as artists I figured selling advertising would at least give me an outlet for my creativity. But I got too attached with my material possessions and found it hard to give up the security of the bi-weekly pay checks. Because I am single and have no one to help pay the bills, I do what I have to keep my artist-self alive. I have to do whatever I can to express the creativity that I am blessed with whether I earn income from it or not.

My current life is pretty close to the ideal life I have always dreamed of. I get up when I wake up. No alarms. I write my morning pages. I eat a healthy breakfast. I walk on the beach with my dog. I write at a local coffee shop. I meet a friend for coffee or lunch or sell advertising for part of the day on the three days of the week that I work. I do pet check in jobs. I teach classes a few times a week. I am in the process of soliciting coaching clients. I meditate daily. I take a yoga class once a week.

It's All About Love

All my life I have felt that I am not quite living up to my potential, that there is a destiny that I need to step into in order to change the world. I have searched and done work to help discover my purpose. But as I face my mortality, I wonder if I will ever realize my purpose. I wonder if I have been fulfilling it all along and haven't realized it—that my purpose, like everyone else's, is simply to love.

At some point, we awaken and become aware that to love is our true purpose. The cancer allowed me to see myself-hatred, to create wars between parts of myself. The divine purpose has been served and I can now drop it. Now I can focus on loving myself just the way I am, cancer or not. Cancer can come back and ravage my body, but it can never touch my spirit. I am a perfect expression of God. The journey is never without challenges that test us and make us doubt our faith. We all have the potential to inflict harm on others. But if we can come back into balance and open up to love again, all will be well.

Seasons

Life is a series of seasons. There will always be ups and downs, joy and sorrow, light and dark, but we can choose to feel joy no matter what season we are in.

The Call

Every day, I pray for discernment of call. I ask for guidance for that day rather than guidance for my whole life. "God, show me your path. Show me what you would have me do."

I have never doubted that God has a purpose for me, one that I am free to ignore, misinterpret or accept. What I don't know is when God will be predisposed to share that purpose with me. First, I had to rid myself of expectations of what I thought a purpose or calling should be.

What I have learned is that God's call tends to be unsurprising and fairly mundane. It can come from everyday avenues such as a phone call or email from a friend or a stranger's plea. It is rarely what I expect, but once I think about what new direction it will take me, the call makes sense. It flows from my authentic self. The call will heal some kind of wound, answer a question, use a life experience, or bridge a chasm and it might lead us to a painful place. Once we accept the call, things change. It is a chain reaction—one choice opens up further choices along the way. God knows we can handle whatever comes even if we deceive ourselves or miss the point, God sees the goodness inside us.

Telling Our Stories

For me it started with an illness that served to tear open the smallness of my life and revealed that something vast was near. All my life I had searched for it. In prayer, in meditation, books, nature, celibacy, obsessive sex and in others. It was in me the whole time. Finally, out of exhaustion, I admitted to myself that I was not the one in control, and I ended my search.

My surroundings are the same. I still worry about paying the bills. But I am happier most of the time. I smile more. I am free. I found love within myself. I am a mystic without a monastery, a light in the darkness. This can mean I smile at a stranger at the store and perhaps change the way their day is going. It can mean changing the way I write in my journal as if writing letters to God. When I feel unafraid to walk in my own skin and am fully who I am without apology, editing, toning down or denying my spirit.

I've been told that I am too serious, too wacky, too honest, and too hard on myself. So I learned to tone it down. I can't do that anymore. I can no longer dim who I am. I am beloved to God simply because I am. So there is no reason I can't love myself the same way. All of myself, even my dark side.

I have been hiding from the truth because if I am fully present in my body, it means I must own just how powerful I am. The responsibility of this seems too overwhelming. I will have to accept that I am worthy of receiving love just because I am me. I don't have to create a cancer in myself to get people to love and pay attention to me.

I don't need cancer to be the true healer I am, who remains the wise sage in the midst of the living dead, those who are not yet awake. But because of the cancer, I no longer see myself as less worthy, less sacred or less loved than those around me. It took me getting cancer to learn to love myself.

I had to get cancer to see that the earth is full of cancer: it comes in the form of self-hatred and people who are separated from God. Because of my journey, I can now be one of the ones to lead people back to love, balance and to the God of their understanding. In this way, cancer is healing humanity. I was also uncomfortable with feminine power and tended not to trust many women. But it was women I turned to when I got ill to ask for help and they were the ones who stepped up. It changed how I viewed women. I now see them as incredibly strong and powerful. I also learned that I am one tough cookie (woman) also. I have tons of compassion. I love being a woman on this earth. Now I can reach out my hand to other women and help them in their time of need. I am no longer a victim of cancer. I chose it to learn what I had forgotten along the way. It is a gift, not only for me but a form of healing for all of humanity. It teaches people to replace self-hatred with self-love.

Cancer is just a word that creates fear. We can choose to focus instead on balancing our bodies and see illness as just symptoms of imbalance.

I feel that I am healing myself from the second bout of cancer so I can continue with my life's work unencumbered. I still have some karma to resolve, and more teaching to do on earth before I graduate to the spiritual place and take my place as a spiritual guide.

The turning point for me is when I began to love, accept and respect myself. It came after years of self-care, which included getting body treatments, EMDR therapy, and exercising. Once you experience unconditional love, it doesn't mean you always feel it. I sometimes have to get myself back there through meditation, spending time with my dog and in nature.

I also did a tremendous amount of healing when I had a session with my friend who is a medium. Not only did my beloved dog, Spark, come through which helped me release much of the guilt and sadness I felt after her death, but my dad came through. He said things to me that I had wanted to hear all my life. He was never very verbal with his feelings when he was alive but in his spiritual form, he was very forthcoming with his love and caring for me.

I hadn't always been close to my dad although I felt like we were a lot alike in many ways. I felt like he tried to get me to conform to his image of who he thought I should be which I rebelled against. But in the spiritual realm, it felt like he was embracing me and so proud of who I was. I finally felt an unconditional love from him. It was like he was giving me permission to be me. This was a necessary step for me in order to be ready to live out my purpose and heal myself. It validated that I was not flawed, but perfect and precious the way I was.

This experience amplified the growing sense I had been cultivating for a while which was a sixth sense beyond my five physical senses. I felt like I owed it to myself and to everyone I met to be my unique, true self. To be inauthentic deprives the universe of my true purpose for being here. Without cancer, I would not have woken up and allowed myself to become my true self again so I could heal myself and others. It showcased the fear I was living with that caused the imbalance in my mind, body and spirit. I am learning to love the cancer because without it, I don't think I would have awakened. Whether using alternative healing methods heal me or not, I believe that letting go and surrendering to God's will is the ultimate healing.

CHAPTER FOURTEEN

Coming Home

What does it mean to come home? For me, it is being in a place where my outside self matches my inside self, when I feel "at home" in my body, in my own skin. It is about loving and adoring myself and not having to do anything or behave in a certain way after years of anxiety, struggle and pain.

Growing up, I never felt like I fit in. I was an artist at heart, a free spirit, but was pushed by my parents to follow a responsible, sensible path. My mom would praise me for my writing ability but the message underneath was that I would never be able to make money at it.

My Dad was a tall, good-looking man who commanded respect from his family and all whom he met. I knew he loved me. I was daddy's little girl. Except he never told my brother and I out loud that he loved us and seemed unable or unwilling to show us much affection. So I spent a good deal of my life trying to win his love and approval; to get him to be proud of me. He was strict and we were expected to follow his rules or pay the consequences- deal with his anger and criticism or spankings, which caused me to feel anxious. My brother and I were both good kids so I never understood why my dad was so angry at us all the time. Now I know it was his own unresolved anger at his own dad.

I found release from being in nature. I would lay on the grass under a huge tree in our yard and just gaze at its strong trunk and branches full of leaves and feel at peace. I also felt peace around the family pets. Both nature and being around animals are very important to me still.

I was brought up as a Christian and went to Bible study as a young child and then didn't return to church until I was 30 years old. I was told I needed to be a "good girl" in order to get to heaven so I always tried to do the right thing and be responsible.

Now I see religion as a path for finding the truth. Different people follow different paths to find their truth and there is not just one path as many would have you believe. The road to getting to this belief was long and difficult and full of wrong turns.

I got married twice and got divorced both times. I never had kids. I never fit the norm and because I didn't fit the standard expected of me, to be a wife and mother, I started to feel like I was flawed.

My Soul's Plan

I don't believe in coincidences. I believe that I was led to every person, step, and resource that was put in my path, at the exact right time and in the right order. First I had to face reality and accept that I had cancer and find out what causes cancer and how to reverse it. I had to move beyond what conventional medicine prescribes to alternative health practices. But even that was not enough. I had to go deeper and come back to God in a true, complete way. To give my life and control completely over to God and live with complete faith and trust.

All the ways I have used to heal myself have aligned with God's natural way of living, but what I was missing was living my life with total faith in God's plan and will.

In order to come home, first you must leave home. This does not necessarily physically mean leaving home, but letting go of what feels safe and known so a new possibility can unfold. What once felt secure is replaced with openness and not knowing. This is a crucial time when we stumble around in the dark to call on God in a new way. I needed to see God as a woman, as a feminist, when for so long men were seen as the source of authority in the spiritual world. Getting cancer propelled me into a totally unknown situation and I had no choice but to open up to God in a whole new, more complete way.

I can best explain it by referring to myths, examples of descents. Innocent young Persephone was abducted by Hades and brought to the underworld. Like her, I had to die to the innocence and security I lived with. The result was being reborn.

Hero's Journey

Whatever position of authority I had in the world became unimportant and useless. It is interesting that I moved from a full-time, stressful sales job where I got commissions that put me at the fore-front to a part-time job where I created and promoted special events and the focus was on the groups and events not me. This process took time. I had to wait on the clues that came to me deep within my cells.

In the descent, I learned to trust the neglected parts of myself, and even love them. Part of the journey required me to come to terms with my own experience so I could cross the threshold and accept my life for what it was.

It was a scary time as it was all new stuff and I didn't have any guidelines. As I let go of old roles and beliefs, there are those who see such a path as foolhardy, even dangerous. I could not please those who asked "why can't you just be satisfied with things as they are?" or "why can't you just keep your full-time job with good benefits?" All I knew was that I could not silence the yearning of my heart and I had to follow my spiritual path above all else, even if it did not make sense to the rest of the world. I had to trust the process itself and let the details fall into place.

The descent included me moving away from my mother, a relationship I thought had nourished me. I found myself increasingly angry and critical with her in order to gather the energy needed to separate from her. I came to a point where I cut off all contact with her so I would not lose all that I had worked so hard for to become healthy and whole.

This time of leaving home requires that we have a tolerance for uncertainty, a capacity to surrender and be able to endure the pressures that occur- economic, social and family.

God used my breast cancer to purify my mind and soul. It led to my spiritual awakening. I had always been a spiritual person. But now my relationship with God became real and personal. Then God led me to share my journey with you. God led you to pick up this book so that you would know that you are not alone.

Just like God did with me, your health will be restored. You will be led to the perfect treatment and resources for you that you will need on your journey with cancer. It is what we do with our suffering that matters and defines who we are. We may not be cured, but we can heal ourselves and become whole.

Even making comprehensive changes in our lifestyle for only three months can cause changes in over five-hundred genes and turns off genes that promote many chronic illnesses.

I don't believe that God gave me cancer but when I got it, God did use it for His purposes. I was led to the right doctor, nurses, MRI scheduler, EMDR therapist, acupuncturist and naturopath. I was led to the right resources so I could understand what was happening to me physically. But in the end, it was God who would decide the outcome.

As I read about what can cause cancer, I got so paranoid, that I was afraid to put anything into my mouth or subject myself to any external toxins. I lived in fear. I wasn't really living. As I learned to trust God completely, I relaxed. I know that if I am to be healed that I don't have to be afraid anymore.

When people would comment on my "positive attitude," I knew the truth. It was the peace and contentment that comes as a result of trusting God. It was an answer to the prayers of so many who chose to stand by me.

Cancer broke my heart wide open which allowed God to penetrate the depths of my heart through the cracks. I trusted God to make me whole again.

For me, a rigid regimen of prayer and bible reading isn't what defines spirituality. I find God in nature, in stranger's smiles, and in meditation.

For me, certain things could only be revealed to me through adversity. How I had put other's first, let my mother's manipulation and guilt trips control my life and my inability to manage stress well. I would not trade my experience for anything. It was through my suffering that God got my undivided attention. The time was used to heal me, to develop my patience and allow me to give faith a chance to work. It is a time of waiting on God's timing. This has been one of the hardest things for me to do as I am impatient. I tend to get resentful when I think I should be rewarded for hard work.

But then I am prompted to take a walk on the beach near my home or hear a beloved song on one of my CD's, or read the perfect quote or book that reminds me I am not in control. God is. God knows the perfect time for everything. The daily challenge for me is to listen to what I am to do for that day, even if it seems to make no worldly sense.

One day, I'll be going along, enjoying the day with no agenda and my life changes. Just like that. In one day. All of a sudden my life is better than I could have imagined or planned. My insides and outside match up and I feel comfortable in my own skin. I am becoming whole and healthy and I am ready to live out my dreams in a more fearless way. There have been times I have thought I was ready to take the fearless leap, only to have to stop and retrace my steps and prepare more thoroughly for the right time. I can't push things. I must wait and let God bear my burdens. My scars from my surgery remind me that I must stay on my knees and trust God.

I have come to believe that I did pre-life planning and have lived many lives on earth. It is the only thing that makes sense to me. I believe that I chose to get cancer twice in order to learn how to love and accept myself. I chose a difficult path so I could be refined into the spiritual leader that I am meant to be. Not until this lifetime do I feel I am that leader and that once I have fulfilled what I am to do, I will no longer have to come back to earth.

I feel like I chose my parents, friends, jobs and everything else so I could learn all the lessons I needed to. Because we have free will, we deviate from the plan. We choose how to react to the challenges we planned with either anger and bitterness or love and compassion. I believe that I chose a highly dysfunctional family so I could appreciate love and compassion more deeply because I didn't receive what I needed from my family.

The very event that caused me suffering is also what ultimately relieved my suffering. It reawakened my passion and is in that way a cause for celebration. As I learned to respond positively to my challenges, I opened an "energetic pathway" that made it easier for others to heal from their challenges. We are all connected through energy. As we raise our frequencies, we emit it into the world. I am learning, through reiki, to open myself up to the world's healing energy and receive it from those who have blazed the trail ahead of me.

I believe I chose in this lifetime to be healed by love. When I can see things this way, I am no longer a victim but am merely following the script I wrote long ago. There is no one to blame. I chose to be a Light worker, or someone whose life is particularly service-oriented and is committed to helping others. That is the primary reason I kept pushing myself to finish this book as I knew it would help many people. I have often been misunderstood. But now as I allow myself to share my light, my true self is emerging and I experience the love that is there for me. I chose cancer so I can remember this love.

Cancer sprang from my thoughts and feelings about myself as I got off my path. I grew up believing that I was unworthy of receiving love so that was the part of me that needed healing. When I got ill, many people came to me with love and support and I was ready to receive it. This love healed my spirit. Those who had been in my life that were unable to give me any love or support were the ones I eliminated from my life. Whether my body is completely healed remains to be seen. But because I believe that I am completely healed and balanced, I believe that it will happen.

The body has one agenda and the soul has another. When I look at things this way, I realize my goal is to raise my consciousness whatever plan I am on. To always grow and learn and explore.

Why Breast Cancer?

When all the love and attention was showered on me when I got cancer I had to finally accept how loved I was and that I was an inspiration to others. That I was a good, loveable person who made a big difference in the world. I also had to learn how to love and mother myself.

Women who develop breast cancer have issues with hope and trust and often suffer from hurt, sorrow and unfinished business. We must learn to care for ourselves before caring for others.

I learned that I am one tough cookie who has a ton of compassion, especially towards other women. I realized I had a lot of physic ability. There is much about myself to love.

My bravery and desire to heal myself were so great that I selected this particular life plan because of the challenges they offered me. It moved me to soul consciousness, a detachment and neutrality that leads to profound peace.

Because I lost several loved ones, including my dad and my beloved dog, Spark, and Janice, I learned about grief and impermanence. I saw loss before as derailment. Now it is see it as a way to help with my life's work, not derail it. Loss is transient. So I teach what I have learned to you- there is no separation. There is only love and service. Nothing else.

A Time of Waiting

Coming home to one's true self is not for the fainthearted. It requires everything we have and facing the darkness. Even though I had been on a spiritual journey for many years and had worked with a spiritual director for over seven years, I had to accept that the life of the spirit is never static. Once God has you in sight, your life will never be the same. You will be presented with new struggles that move you towards growth, healing and wholeness.

I had to let go of my false selves—good little girl, nice person and victim—and discover who I was at a deep, soul level: the authentic self

God created me to be. I had a constant compulsion reminding me to be "nice" as I was brought up to be instead of being who I really was and doing what I felt like doing. Therefore, I never really learned to trust my feelings until I went into therapy. I discovered that my real work was to free my feelings, to get to know and trust them. I started writing this book hoping to help others through their journey with cancer. But it was I who was healed and changed as I grew to love what I had long denied in myself.

Whatever our mission, whatever the motive that leads us to action, it moves us to the edge of the cliff. We leave the ground and dare to jump and the angels who watch over us use their wings to soften our fall. It was not just the writing of the book for me. It was an honest conversation with my mother that had been long suppressed.

We become ill when we become unbalanced, or when we allow our fears and ego to edge God out of our lives. When we come back (come home) to God, in our body, mind and soul, we then experience first-hand the words of Jesus, that "with God all things are possible." It is then that hope replaces fear.

It is up to us to banish all disease-producing thoughts from our lives, so that God can heal every part of us. Whatever path feels right to you personally, the path you believe will heal you, is the right path for you. But because of expectations from family, friends and culture, we start to pretend to be something we are not in order to fit in or to not make waves or cause problems. I got caught up in this more than once and went through a period of being afraid of everything that could possibly cause cancer to re- occur which led to fearing life itself. But just when fear began to rule my life, I would be led to a new person, resource, belief and would be reminded that God was always inside me and I had nothing to fear.

I discovered that I had to live the question, listen and be patient. From the time of waiting comes creativity. It's a slow process that can't be rushed. Just as a butterfly can't be forced out of its cocoon, we can't force our time of waiting for God's guidance. When I get impatient and try and take shortcuts, I have to go back and take the long way around; the deep, more arduous, inward path.

Growth is a continuous, life-long process. I believe that God healed me of my cancer but it did not happen in an instant. It took me doing my part to heal myself. I waited actively versus waiting passively. What I have found to be of most importance is what I put into my mouth. I have tried to be more of a vegetarian but believe that God wants me to eat food only in its natural form, as God intended, and to remove all toxins, hormone-enhanced and chemically altered foods from my diet.

God's word, as I understand it as a Christian feminist, is the foundation for total, whole being. What thoughts I put into my brain, my beliefs, causes what I do and the things I put into my body, and mind. When I started believing that I was well and gave thanks to God for all the moments of well-being I experienced, I began to get well. But I still had to do my part by eating right and exercising. I needed to include daily exercise, prayer, meditation and right thinking into my life.

I have gone from one extreme to the other, from being mindless about my health and distant from God to becoming obsessive about doing all the "right" things to heal myself. I have come to center and am more relaxed. I give God the control. I do my part. I am no longer frightened that I will get cancer back. If it does, then I will deal with it then. The feelings of well-being well outweigh the feelings of fear and anger.

As I did my research for this book, I read how surgery is not effective in getting rid of the cancer. It gets rid of the tumor, but not the cancer process. In fact, surgery is what can cause metaosis- spreading the cancer throughout the body. I started beating myself up for getting the surgery. But then I was led to a book by a mind-body physician and it helped me re-frame my surgery. I believe that my doctor was a true healer and that God put me in good hands. Because I believed that she was good at what she did and that the surgery worked, it did.

I didn't want a foreign substance (tumor) inside of me, so I had to get it out for my peace of mind. My doctor listened, opened her heart, made eye contact and used touch to calm me. She invited me to be her partner and let me know that we would make decisions together to get me well. She educated, not dictated. She phrased her words to be optimistic: "You *will* survive this." But most of all, she offered hope.

I have found that when I gather up my courage and reveal my light (the spiritual power given to me by God), I set myself up for being attacked by evil and dark forces. People who do not choose to share their own light. When I get afraid, all I can do is give my fears to God. Fear is not from God. My beloved Spark, who passed away about a year ago, taught me what it must be like to have God love me. My current dog, Brodie, loves me unconditionally also. But I can no longer limit myself to the love of my dogs. I must surrender to God's enormous love of me which gives me a supernatural peace that can't be explained or earned.

I get back to the certainty that I must finish this book and it will get published if it is meant to so it can help others heal.

Getting Lost in Order to be Found

Love Letter to God

Too long in the wilderness
Has made me into a prodigal daughter
Wandering in the desert
Too lost to find my way.
I have reached a dead end
With nowhere else to turn.
I meet you in the inner sanctuary
Where you have been waiting for me all along
Do I need to make amends for my long absence?
Or do I seek the comfort of your arms?
I love you God.
I am waiting for your answer.

Somewhere along the way, I got confused. I got side-tracked from my faith and I became the center of my universe. I worked hard at staying in control of every aspect of my life and I lost my balance. I started thinking I could shape and control God. Cancer allowed me to let God be God and to allow God to shape and mold me.

To let life happen and unfold is exceedingly hard and very hard to explain to those who are constantly striving. I noticed that the more I let go of the need to control things, the more relaxed, calm and at peace I became and people started commenting on this.

I still have goals and desires for the future, but I have given up my need to control and manipulate in order to reach them. Through therapy, I learned that facing my pain would not kill me. Running away only made things worse. I had to finally face the pain.

Religion helps me put words to my spirituality/faith. When it comes down to it all I want is God, in whatever way God comes, even if it is painful. No one can help us decide how to live our life. There are no guarantees or certainty. As I learn to let go of the illusion of control and trust myself and trust that there is something beyond what I can see, my life becomes calmer. I become more at peace. Am I willing to risk the unknown in order to find my way? Yes. Am I willing to let go of the critic inside that tries to keep me from loving myself? Yes. This time, I make the choice to follow what I truly want. God. Fear will have to make this journey without me.

At some point, we must surrender to the experience and descend into one's interior depths. Then we must call on God and wait. Relax into the storm swirling around and inside us. It is an active waiting. We look for clues on the meaning of the storm, crisis, so we can transcend it. God doesn't cause the crisis, or illness, but uses it. I could no longer run away from death. I had to face that I would die physically someday and let my old selves die away. I looked death in the face and said, "I want to live! But if I die, I die. And it will all be well whatever happens. I will be ok."

My journey with cancer helped me reach a point where I needed to question my faith, face my doubts and see God in a new way so I could keep growing. So my faith is true to where I am now in my life.

Radical Self-care

Radical self-care means shifting from a self-centered focus to a more God-centered focus. It is a winding, spiraling, complicated process.

An example is separating myself from my dysfunctional family as the pain of relating to them became too painful and required me to be make myself small. I feared that if I let them go, I would have no love in my life, no one to depend on. But the truth is there was a greater love out there for me outside my family.

For me, radical self-care includes eating a "flexitarian" diet (primarily vegetarian with some organic, free-range chicken), using negative language if I feel like it like "fuck the cancer!" I make the rules.

Healing on My Own Terms

Traditional health care focuses on cure and disease management. Healing involves being aligned in our body, mind and spirit. There is no cure yet for cancer and there is no guarantee you will be healed. It requires our active participation. I made a decision early on to not be involved in long-term management of the cancer but I have always wanted healing. I still had a lot to love for and was not going to stop doing whatever I could in order to find healing.

Becoming

My prayer is to become all that you envision
To be fully myself
To accept all that I am.
Walk with me to the edge God
Beyond all security
Take me to where courage lies
And release me to become.

About a year after my mastectomy, I had a vivid dream. I heard noises in the basement of the house I was in and went to explore. The garage door was open. Lights were on as if someone was making themselves at home. Out of the corner of my eye, I saw a man scurry out the garage door to the outdoors. He kept looking back at my dog and me. My dog was barking like crazy at the intruder, protecting me from the evil presence. My words were stuck in my throat. I could not yell at him to go away. I had to let go and trust that my dog and I would be safe.

Coming Home

As stillness comes at day's end
Thoughts crowd my mind
Despair and pity skirt the edges
The pain and suffering
Threaten to overtake my heart
The years of being unbalanced
Of being someone other than my true self
Have made me someone I no longer recognize.
Walking through the refuse left by discarded masks,
I stumble over the one thing I need in order to get back to center
A place of faith, of hope, of stillness
I close my eyes and drop off to sleep
Knowing that protective wings surround me.

As we come back to earth in a different body, we soon begin to forget that the earth is not our true home. Heaven, the spiritual realm, is our true home. We live in our bodies and become emotionally involved with everything that happens on earth. It becomes harder to let go the longer we are here. In my journey, I am becoming more focused on how wonderful heaven, my true home, is. I don't feel I will come back to earth as a human being. Once I accomplish what I am here to do, I will be free to graduate to the spiritual realm.

Surrender

I had climbed the mountain. I was over the top. I was coming alive again. I had survived the toughest time in my life. It was finally okay to relax. It was okay to celebrate being alive. Then I fell back off the top of the mountain when I faced cancer a second time. Did I want to make the effort to climb to the top again? I had to make the decision again if I really wanted to live.

I decided I wanted to, but this time I wanted to live well and to live fully, always knowing that death could happen at any moment. And this time, I couldn't do it alone. I had to ask for help. A sweetness and joy are present even in the challenges. I dare to love so profoundly that I build bridges to other human beings.

Recently, I saw the movie "Gravity" with Sandra Bullock. It affected me deeply. I observed her face her moment of truth, her own "hero's journey," when she let go of the past and decided to live and do what it took to get home to earth. She realized that she had two possible outcomes: to crash and die in outer space, or to survive and have a story to tell. She was ready for whatever was to come. She was ready for one hell of a ride.

You experience the worst thing that can happen and you aren't sure you want to keep living without that being. So you have one foot in Heaven so you can be with your beloved. You have to make a choice. You don't know the outcome of that choice as you are not in control. But if you choose to fight for your life, you use whatever resources you have to survive. You listen to your intuition, you use critical thinking skills, and you pray and ask God for guidance. You don't ever give up. And if you do indeed survive, you are grateful and you share your story.

I look back on my experience with the MRI and the terror I felt and now I know it sprang from my fear of being out of control, an inability to escape. Because of the journey that cancer has taken me on, I now believe in freedom from fear. I believe in bravery and courage and facing the darkness and the fear. I believe in acquiring the skills to force the bad out of the world so that the good can prosper and thrive.

I choose to live and to heal myself. Whatever happens, I am ready for one hell of a ride.

ENDNOTES

Chapter One

1. Gail Godwin, *The Finishing School* (New York, NY: Random House, 1999), 254.
2. Kahlil Gibran, *The Prophet.* (New York, New York: Alfred & Knopp, 1923). 129.

Chapter Four

1. Louise L. Hay, *You Can Heal Your Life* (Carlsbad, CA: Hay House, 1999), 8.
2. Raymond M. Francis, MSC, *Never Fear Cancer Again: How to prevent and reverse cancer* (Deerfield, FL, Health Communications, 2011), 63-65.
3. Raymond M. Francis, MSC, *Never Fear Cancer Again: How to prevent and reverse cancer* (Deerfield, FL, Health Communications, 2011), 63-65.

Chapter Six

1. Bernie S. Siegel, M.D., *Love, Medicine & Miracles* (Novato, CA, New World Communications, 1998), 6.

Chapter Seven

1. Sue Fredericks, *I See Your Dream Job: A career intuitive shows you how to discover what you were put on earth to do* (New York, NY: St Martin's Press, 2009), 41.

Chapter Eight

1. Parker J. Palmer, *The Courage to Teach: Exploring the inner landscape of a teacher's life.* (1st ed.) (San Francisco, CA: Jossey-Bass., 1998), 173-189.

Chapter Nine

1. Margery Williams, *The Velveteen Rabbit* (Kansas City, MS: Andrews& McNeel, 1991), p.2

Chapter Eleven

1. Raymond M. Francis, MSC, *Never Fear Cancer Again: How to prevent and reverse cancer* (Deerfield, FL, Health Communications, 2011), 63-65.
2. Raymond M. Francis, MSC, *Never Fear Cancer Again: How to prevent and reverse cancer* (Deerfield, FL, Health Communications, 2011), 63-65.

Chapter Thirteen

1. Sue Fredericks, *I See Your Dream Job: A career intuitive shows you how to discover what you were put on earth to do* (New York, NY: St Martin's Press, 2009), 41.

Edwards Brothers Malloy
Oxnard, CA USA
December 31, 2015